Quiet-Time
Prayers
for a
Teen Girl's
Heart

Hilary Bernstein

Quiet-Time
Prayers
for a
Teen Girl's Heart

180
Comforting
Conversations
with God

BARBOUR
PUBLISHING

Published by Barbour Publishing, Inc., 1810 Barbour Drive, Uhrichsville, Ohio 44683, www.barbourbooks.com

Our mission is to inspire the world with the life-changing message of the Bible.

Member of the
Evangelical Christian
Publishers Association

Printed in the United States of America.

Introduction

If you ever feel like you're constantly bombarded by messages and opinions and requests, it's because you are. So much in this world fights for your attention. You may get used to all the noise and not even realize how much it adds stress and drags you down. But when you take time for your Creator, you can watch your worries melt away. His still, small voice won't demand your attention, but He is always ready to communicate with you.

The prophet Elijah experienced this in 1 Kings 19. Elijah knew the Lord would pass by. A huge wind blew, but the Lord wasn't in the wind. After the wind, an earthquake came, then a fire. But the Lord wasn't in the earthquake or the fire. Only when Elijah heard the sound of a gentle blowing did he know the Lord had arrived.

Like Elijah's experience, the Lord won't come in the noise or chaos of this world. But when you take time to get away with Him, He'll touch your heart. He'll reveal His truth to you through His Word and you'll be able to communicate with Him through prayer. When you slow down enough to quiet your words and your thoughts, He'll fill you with amazing things like His peace and joy. Relish the comfort only He can bring!

Come to Me

"Come to Me, all who are weary and burdened,
and I will give you rest. Take My yoke upon you
and learn from Me, for I am gentle and humble
in heart, and you will find rest for your souls."

MATTHEW 11:28–29 NASB

Lord God Almighty, knowing that You invite me to come
to You is such a relief. I don't have to get my act together
ahead of time. I don't need to pretend I'm someone I'm
not. I can forget about being perfect. I can come to You
just as I am, broken and imperfect and confused. I can
bring You all my worries and doubts and fears, and You'll
willingly take them from me. Sometimes I feel so weighed
down by all that's on my mind and in my heart. But when I
come to You and give You all my concerns, You promise to
give my soul rest. You'll fill me with Your peace. From the
inside out, You'll give me strength to keep going. Thank
You! In Jesus' name I pray. Amen.

Growing in Wisdom

For wisdom is better than jewels; and all
desirable things cannot compare with her.
PROVERBS 8:11 NASB

Heavenly Father, a lot of things in this world vie for my attention. It's easy to get caught up in focusing on belongings or popularity or how well I'm doing. But when I think of You and what Your Word teaches, I don't have to worry about those things. What I really need in whatever I face is wisdom. Could You please help me grow in Your wisdom? Proverbs promises that wisdom is more valuable than jewels. The thing is, I don't know how to be wise on my own. You are wise though. Because of that, I pray You'll fill me with Your wisdom so I can have a better perspective and understanding of this life. I'd be lost without You. In Jesus' name I pray. Amen.

At Peace

Now that we have been made right with God by
putting our trust in Him, we have peace with Him.
It is because of what our Lord Jesus Christ did for us.
ROMANS 5:1 NLV

Lord, more than anything else I'd like to be made right with You! I don't want to be at odds with You. I love You and want to give my life to You and You alone. To do that, I need to trust You completely. And I do! I put my trust in Jesus. Thank You for the peace Jesus brings. Thank You for the way He came to earth as a rescuer. Trusting Him completely seems like a big request because I'm surrendering absolutely everything to Him. Yet it's such a simple thing to do. I don't have to worry about working hard or achieving peace with You on my own. That comes through Jesus. He did the work, and because of that, He is more than worthy of my trust. Thank You for Jesus! Thank You for the way He makes me right with You! I love You.

Who Am I?

When I consider your heavens, the work of your fingers, the moon and the stars, which you have set in place, what is mankind that you are mindful of them, human beings that you care for them?

PSALM 8:3-4 NIV

Lord God, You are amazing! I admit that I need to stand in awe of You more often. You've created absolutely everything, from astounding wonders like the ocean and mountains and the starry night sky, to tiny miracles like insects and seeds and cells in my body. What You've done is way more than I can begin to comprehend. I worship You for Your greatness. I worship You for Your majesty and power. And I thank You that out of all creation, You chose to make humans in Your own image. Not only were we made in Your image, but You chose to care for us too. Who am I to receive Your loving care? Thank You for Your kindness! Thank You for meeting my needs day after day. You are so very good to me. I don't even want to imagine what life would be like without Your generosity. Thank You!

Gathered and Carried

*He tends his flock like a shepherd: He gathers the
lambs in his arms and carries them close to his heart.*
ISAIAH 40:11 NIV

Heavenly Father, I need a shepherd to lead and guide me.
Sometimes I feel a little lost in this world. Knowing You'll
care for my every need and carry me close to Your heart
is such a huge relief and comfort. Trying to do everything
on my own and making my own big decisions is hard!
Knowing what is a right or wrong choice can be confusing.
Making and relying on my decisions is overwhelming. I
want to remember You're just like a good shepherd. You
know where I'm headed, and You want to keep me close
by Your side. Please lead me through life in an abundantly
clear way. I want to listen to You and Your direction! When
I'm worn out by life, I pray I'll come to You for comfort. I
know You'll gather me in Your arms and carry me because
You are my good, good Father. I love You!

The Sunrise from On High

"Because of the tender mercy of our God, with which the Sunrise from on high will visit us, to shine on those who sit in darkness and the shadow of death, to guide our feet into the way of peace."

LUKE 1:78–79 NASB

Lord God, when I watch the sun rise in the morning, I'm in awe. As the Master Artist, You paint the sky in such beautiful colors. What once was covered in darkness is made bright and visible. The way stunning daily sunrises can show me so much about what's to come is amazing. This world is a dark place without Christ. Without Him, people stumble in darkness. No wonder there's so much evil and confusion! But Christ is the light. He's the Sunrise from on high. He visited earth to rescue souls from the shadow of death. Thank You for sending Him! Thank You for Your mercy! Thank You for the way You guide my feet into the way of peace. I pray Your Sunrise will shine in my heart and my life. Please brighten my mind to Your ways and shine Your truth into the corners and crevices of my life. In Jesus' name I pray. Amen.

No Worries

"They will be like a tree planted by the water that sends out its roots by the stream. It does not fear when heat comes; its leaves are always green. It has no worries in a year of drought and never fails to bear fruit."
JEREMIAH 17:8 NIV

Lord, when I look at all that's happening in the world around me, it's easy to get distracted and discouraged. Worries and fears seem natural. But when I remain close to You, I don't have to be distracted by the world's troubles. I don't have to worry. I don't have to fear when troubles start heating up. Instead, when I trust in You, I can be like a tree planted by streams of water. I'll be nourished by You and rooted in Your truth. You'll keep me blooming and growing even when it seems like everything around me is parched and dry. When I stay connected to You by prayer and reading Your Word, I'll bear fruit. Thank You for refreshing me and keeping me nourished and nurtured. You are so good to me! In Jesus' name I pray. Amen.

God's Good Plan

For I am confident of this very thing, that
He who began a good work among you will
complete it by the day of Christ Jesus.
PHILIPPIANS 1:6 NASB

Father God, it's amazing to know that You've started a good work in me and You've planned how You'll work in my life. Who am I to deserve Your love and kindness and attention? Clearly I can see moments when You're doing really great things in me and through me. That is so exciting! And at other times, I feel like I get in Your way. Please help me trust You more and more each day. Please help me follow Your lead. Sometimes it seems like I need You to use a megaphone! I want to carefully listen for Your voice and Your direction. As You guide me, please help me bravely step out in faith to follow Your very good plans for my life. I know I can trust You! In Jesus' name I pray. Amen.

Strength and Peace

The LORD will give strength to His people;
the LORD will bless His people with peace.

PSALM 29:11 NASB

Lord, thank You for Your really good gifts! You know me better than I know myself, and You know I sometimes feel weak. Thank You for giving me strength! And thank You for blessing me with peace. You have a wonderful way of taking away my fears and filling me with Your peace. Instead of dwelling on what might happen, I want to dwell on You instead. When I consider You instead of what is going on around me, my perspective shifts. You offer me peace. You offer to turn my weakness into strength when I depend on You. I pray I'll stop trying to do things in my own power or with my own ideas and instead rely on You. You're more than worthy of my trust and reliance! In Jesus' name I pray. Amen.

Don't Give Up

"As for you, be strong and do not give up,
for your work will be rewarded."
2 CHRONICLES 15:7 NIV

Father, sometimes I'm tempted to give up. When challenges come and I face opposition—whether people give me a hard time or circumstances seem too difficult—it's hard to keep going. Resistance feels uncomfortable, and I don't always feel like fighting through difficulties. But I need to remember that endurance is a really good thing. Perseverance feels so hard, but it's the best thing to do. As I wait and endure and persevere, could You please help me? Please strengthen me so I don't give up. Please help me keep going so I can experience a reward. As I endure with strength, please help me take the next step so I can continue to do the right thing, step-by-step. I may not have the strength to do everything right now, but with You and Your help, I can do the *next* right thing. Thank You for never leaving me on my own. I love You!

Lots of Love

Our Lord Jesus Christ and God our Father loves us.
Through His loving-favor He gives us comfort and
hope that lasts forever. May He give your hearts
comfort and strength to say and do every good thing.
2 THESSALONIANS 2:16–17 NLV

Lord Jesus, You have given me so many wonderful things.
Thank You! With Your great love and favor, You've filled
me with comfort. You've given me hope that lasts forever.
You comfort my heart in a way that nothing or no one else
can. And You fill me with Your strength so I can say and do
good things. Apart from You, I could try to find comfort,
hope, and strength. I could try to say and do every good
thing on my own. But You know I wouldn't get very far!
I really need Your help, and I'm especially thankful for
the ways You fill my life with Your goodness. I don't deserve
any of this, so I appreciate the way You love me. Please
help me live my life in such a way that will show You how
much I love You. In Your name I pray. Amen.

There Is Hope!

"If you set your heart right, and put out your hands to Him. . . Your life would be brighter than noon. Darkness would be like the morning. Then you would trust, because there is hope. You would look around and rest and be safe."

JOB 11:13, 17–18 NLV

Father, so many good things come when I trust You. You brighten my life and You clearly show me Your way. I can rest in You because You keep me safe. When I try to do things in my own strength or by my own way of thinking, I don't experience Your peace. I don't have so much clarity. Sometimes I feel like I'm wandering around in the dark instead of Your brightness. Instead of relying on myself, I want to set my heart right and turn to You. I open my hands to You. Please lead and guide me in Your way. Please show me Your truth and let it change my heart and mind. Thank You for true hope that comes only from You. And thank You for Your peace that's so much greater than anything I can understand. In Jesus' name I pray. Amen.

No Confusion

For God is not a God of confusion, but of peace.
1 CORINTHIANS 14:33 NASB

Lord God, I love the fact that You are not a God of confusion. At creation You brought chaos into order. You bring clarity into the world and into my life. You have a clear plan and direction for everyone. When I turn to You, You'll fill me with Your peace. This is such a great gift! I hate the way I feel when I'm confused. It never seems right to feel mixed up and out of sorts. I don't like having scattered thoughts. To know that You never experience any of that confusion is amazing. You are a God of order and peace and clarity. What a relief! Could You please share some of that with me? Please fill me with Your peace and direct my paths. I'd love Your clear direction in my life. You are so awesome and amazing. I worship You!

Waiting in Hope

We wait in hope for the LORD; he is our help and our shield. In him our hearts rejoice, for we trust in his holy name. May your unfailing love be with us, LORD, even as we put our hope in you.

PSALM 33:20–22 NIV

Lord, I admit that waiting is really hard for me to do. I get impatient and antsy. I want things to happen right away. It's difficult to wait and see what You'll do or how You'll answer my prayers. Yet You are my help. You are my protection. I can put all of my trust in You and Your holy name. My heart can and should rejoice in You. You love me so faithfully. And when I do put my hope and trust in You, I can wait for You to work out Your perfect plans. I don't have to rush ahead and try to make things happen. I don't have to take control and get my own agenda done. Instead, I want to look to You while I wait for You and Your direction. I want to hope in You and You alone. In Jesus' name I pray. Amen.

Do Not Fear

*This is what the L*ORD *says, He who is your Creator, Jacob, and He who formed you, Israel: "Do not fear, for I have redeemed you; I have called you by name; you are Mine! When you pass through the waters, I will be with you; and through the rivers, they will not overflow you. When you walk through the fire, you will not be scorched, nor will the flame burn you. For I am the L*ORD *your God, the Holy One of Israel, your Savior."*

ISAIAH 43:1–3 NASB

Lord God, time and time again You reminded Israel that You called them and cared for them in amazing ways. They were Your chosen people, and You treated them with favor. In my life, You've created me. You've formed me. And through Christ, You've called me and redeemed me. You've also chosen me. Thank You! I don't have to fear anything in this life, because I'm Yours. You're with me when I'm walking through the storms or fiery trials of this life. I don't have to worry about drowning in bad things that happen. And I don't have to fear getting scorched. You've promised to be with me. I'm Yours. Thank You!

Listen!

"The Holy Spirit is coming. He will lead you into all truth. He will not speak His Own words. He will speak what He hears. He will tell you of things to come."
JOHN 16:13 NLV

Father God, during His time on earth, Jesus promised that the Holy Spirit would come once He left. And after Jesus died, rose from the dead, and then returned to heaven, Your Holy Spirit did come and fill believers. Just as He became part of early believers, He's part of me too, when I believe all that Christ said and did. And when Your Holy Spirit is part of me, He leads me in a gentle but mighty way. Please help me pay attention to Him! When I sense that He's leading and guiding me, I want to be obedient. Help me step out in faith and follow. As He speaks what He hears from You, please help me hear and understand. I want to trust that His leading is right. I want to do Your will, even if I need to boldly step out in faith. You're preparing me for an adventure You've planned just for me. Thank You. I love You!

Rest

"Remember the word which Moses the servant of the Lord commanded you, saying, 'The Lord your God is giving you rest, and will give you this land.'"
JOSHUA 1:13 NASB

Lord God, rest is a wonderful thing. You know that it is, and You know how desperately humans need it. You created everything in six days but rested on the seventh. You didn't need to rest—You're God!—but You knew humans would need rest. You give rest in an amazing and refreshing way. Jesus also promised, "Come to Me, all who are weary and burdened, and I will give You rest" (Matthew 11:28). I don't have to be so concerned about doing and achieving and working hard. I don't have to work until I'm weary or feel like I'm bearing a burden. I can trust that You'll do what You need to do through me. I can rest in that and trust You to accomplish things. I don't know how You work through me, but I know You do. I want to stop worrying and trust You completely. Please help me to rest in You. In Jesus' name I pray. Amen.

The Anchor of My Soul

This hope we have as an anchor of the soul, a hope both sure and reliable and one which enters within the veil, where Jesus has entered as a forerunner for us, having become a high priest forever according to the order of Melchizedek.

HEBREWS 6:19–20 NASB

Father, so often life in this world leaves me feeling like I've been tossed around. All the uncertainty leaves me feeling scared or worried. But I don't need to feel like a toy boat being tossed around in a stormy ocean. I'm actually safe and secure because of Jesus. When I put all my hope and trust in Him, He becomes the anchor of my soul. He keeps me firmly in place, even in the rockiest, stormiest moments of life. I might feel the waves, but I won't be wrecked. I'm so grateful that I can live with certainty and peace because of my faith and trust in Jesus. In the moments when I'm tempted to doubt or fear, please remind me of my soul's anchor. Please remind me of all the wonderful things Jesus has done for me out of His great love. In His name I pray. Amen.

Lifting My Head

You, LORD, are a shield around me,
my glory, the One who lifts my head high.

PSALM 3:3 NIV

Lord, when I'm afraid or start to worry, it's easy to look down. Either I try to mind my own business or I just don't want to see people looking at me. It crushes me to see someone else making fun of me or bullying me. But You're my protector. In fact, You protect me like a shield! And You are my glory. I don't have to worry about myself—from what I look like to how well I do things—because You're the One at work. And when I trust You completely, You'll shine through me. Because You're the One who lifts my head high, I don't have to look down in shame. In You I can be completely secure and confident. Thank You for Your constant protection. I praise You for being my glory! In Your holy name I pray. Amen.

Going before Me

The LORD was going before them in a pillar of
cloud by day to lead them on the way, and in
a pillar of fire by night to give them light, so
that they might travel by day and by night.
EXODUS 13:21 NASB

Lord, You faithfully led the Israelites through the desert for forty years. You never failed them. In fact, You led them all the time—by cloud during the daytime and by fire during the night. Please help me remember that You gently yet distinctly lead me. I may not see a cloud or a flame, but if I pay close attention, You do lead me. I can see Your guidance and direction in what people say to me, in situations, or in the timing of circumstances. Your hand is at work! And even though many days I'd like Your guidance to be as obvious as fire or a cloud, help me seek You and Your will through prayer. You do go before me and prepare my way. You do get things ready in advance. That's pretty amazing, and I'm thankful for that. I want to look for You more and more every day. I want to follow the path You have prepared for me. I trust You completely! In Jesus' name I pray. Amen.

Showing Respect

I urge, then, first of all, that petitions, prayers,
intercession and thanksgiving be made for all people—
for kings and all those in authority, that we may live
peaceful and quiet lives in all godliness and holiness.

1 TIMOTHY 2:1–2 NIV

Father, sometimes I don't like the rule of authorities. I don't like someone else telling me what to do, even if I know it's for my own good. Please help me realize that You're the One who puts authorities in place. You've chosen who will rule and guide. Whether I may agree with my rulers or not, please help me respect them with my attitude and actions. Help me remember to pray for them, that they might lead well and make wise decisions. Thank You that I'm not the boss of everyone. Please help me to be a good follower of elected leaders as long as that doesn't mean disobeying a higher law put in place by You. Instead of being rude and unruly, please help me to live a peaceful and quiet life that glorifies You. I want my life to reflect You. In Jesus' name I pray. Amen.

Kept and Hidden

Keep me as the apple of your eye; hide me in the shadow of your wings from the wicked who are out to destroy me, from my mortal enemies who surround me.

PSALM 17:8–9 NIV

Father God, I'm not entirely sure why not everyone likes me, but it's obvious they don't. It hurts to know people don't like me, and I feel really bad when I realize I have enemies. Please reveal if I've sinned against these people or if I'm innocent and free from blame. Please show me if we only have personality conflicts or if I need to correct and change something in my own life. Because I'll always experience conflict in this life, I pray I'll run to You for protection. I don't want to worry about problems, and I don't want to try to solve things in my own strength. Instead, I want to run to You. Please hide me in the shadow of Your wings. And keep me as the apple of Your eye. I know You love me and want what's best for me. Please work through these uncomfortable situations so I become more and more like You. In Jesus' name I pray. Amen.

Multiplied Goodness

*To those who are the called, beloved in God
the Father, and kept for Jesus Christ: May
mercy, peace, and love be multiplied to you.*

JUDE 1:1-2 NASB

Lord, when I think of all the goodness You offer me, I'm truly amazed. You give me so much more than I can earn or achieve on my own. You've called me to be Your own. You're kind, compassionate, and forgiving. You love me so patiently and generously. Your love always protects, trusts, hopes, and perseveres. And You're keeping me for Jesus Christ. Even if I don't feel like I deserve all of this, You're ready and willing to multiply Your mercy, peace, and love just for me. Some days I can't help but notice what's going wrong, either in my life or in the world around me. I want to start focusing on all the good You have for me. Please help me recognize Your good gifts, fully appreciate them, then thank You for them. I'm truly grateful for all of Your goodness! In Jesus' name I pray. Amen.

My Hiding Place

You are my hiding place; you will protect me from
trouble and surround me with songs of deliverance.

PSALM 32:7 NIV

Father, some days I'd like to curl up into a tiny ball and escape from reality. Sometimes I'm in the middle of a bad day when everything seems to be going wrong, and sometimes the future seems bleak. I imagine all sorts of troubles and bad things that could happen. The amazing thing I need to remember is that You are my hiding place. You'll protect me from trouble. You'll rescue me from despair. Even on my worst days, I can totally put my trust in You because I know You'll work out all the details for my good. Even if I need to learn a hard lesson, You'll protect me. Even if it seems like situations are hopeless, there's always hope with You. Thank You for the way You always look out for me and keep me safe in You. In Jesus' name I pray. Amen.

He'll Never Get Tired

Do you not know? Have you not heard? The LORD is the everlasting God, the Creator of the ends of the earth. He will not grow tired or weary, and his understanding no one can fathom. He gives strength to the weary and increases the power of the weak.

ISAIAH 40:28–29 NIV

Creator God, You are awesome and limitless. When I think of how tired I get, either when I work really hard or don't get enough sleep, it's amazing to realize You never ever get tired or weary. Absolutely nothing wears You out. You created all things, and in You everything is held together. When I do get tired, You'll give me strength. When I feel so weak and small, You'll increase my power in a miraculous way. Because of You, I'll always have strength. I'll always have hope to carry on, because You are my hope and You are my strength. I may not understand how or why You are the way You are, but I don't have to understand. I can appreciate You for the amazing God You are. I worship You!

Hope to Honor

I hope very much that I will have no reason to be ashamed. I hope to honor Christ with my body if it be by my life or by my death. I want to honor Him without fear, now and always.

PHILIPPIANS 1:20 NLV

Lord Jesus, You have done so very much for me. You willingly left Your heavenly home to come to earth, live a sinless life, then die a painful death. You came back to life three days later, showed Your risen, living self to hundreds and hundreds of people, and then You went into heaven. You did all of those miraculous things with complete love. You called me to believe in You, and once I did, I could spend eternity with You. Because of Your great gifts and great sacrifice, I want my entire life to honor You. I want my thoughts, actions, and words to show how much I adore and respect You. I don't want to do anything that would dishonor You. When I'm tempted to sin, please help me remember I'm Yours. Please help me stand firm for You. In Your great name I pray. Amen.

Pleasing to the Lord

The religious leader said to them, "Go in peace.
The way you are going is pleasing to the Lord."
JUDGES 18:6 NLV

Lord, I love You, and I'm thankful that You're my God. Help me please You in all I say and do. When I make decisions each day, guide my choices. I want my choices to point to the fact that I'm Your daughter. As I do follow You, I pray You'll fill me with Your Spirit and help me live out Your love, joy, and peace. Please help me to be patient with others. I want to grow to become a kind woman who is good, faithful, and gentle. Please help me live a life of self-control. I could try all of this on my own and only get frustrated with my failures and sins. But if You're working through me, I know You can do anything. As You live and work in me, I pray that I'm pleasing in Your sight! Help me to know the difference between what is right and wrong, as well as the subtle difference between what is right and what is almost right. I want to please You! In Your name I pray. Amen.

Choosing a Friendship

*Do you not know that to love the sinful things
of the world and to be a friend to them is to
be against God? Yes, I say it again, if you are
a friend of the world, you are against God.*

JAMES 4:4 NLV

Father, temptation is a powerful thing. You know this because humans have been dealing with it ever since Eve was tempted in the garden of Eden. This world is filled with really enticing temptations. Yet no matter how compelling my temptations might feel, help me recognize that when I choose to sin, it really means I'm choosing against You. The more I choose to give in to the temptations of this world, the more I choose to step away from You. It may be hard to stand against the sinful things, but it all comes down to a matter of devotion. Am I devoted to You? Do I really, actually love You? If I do, I want and need to choose You. If I'm not loyal to You, I'll cave in to the world's pressures and pleasures. Please help me understand when I'm running closely with You and when I'm starting to drift away from You. I don't want to be a friend of the world. Please help me see the sinful thoughts, patterns, and actions so I can flee from them. I want to be Your friend!

In Pursuit of Peace

Turn from evil and do good; seek peace and pursue it.
PSALM 34:14 NIV

Father, I know my good deeds won't save me. Only Jesus can do that. But I do pray that I will be good and do good things. In fact, I wish I'd be known for my kindness and for the way I help make other people's days better. When I'm tempted to react in frustration, anger, or revenge, please stop me in my tracks. Help me recognize evil and turn from it. Please give me ideas so I can do good. And Lord, I pray that I'll seek peace with everyone. Even when people are mean or nasty, help me pursue peace with them. Even when my feelings get hurt, I pray I'll rise above whatever is getting me down and seek peace. This isn't easy, and it doesn't come naturally. But with You and Your help, I can do hard things. Please help me to be good and to seek peace! In Jesus' name I pray. Amen.

Success

So Potiphar left everything he had in Joseph's care; with Joseph in charge, he did not concern himself with anything except the food he ate.
GENESIS 39:6 NIV

Lord God, I appreciate the way You've included stories of real men and women in the Bible. I can relate to the way lives have twists and turns. Not everything goes perfectly and smoothly. In fact, many times life is filled with unexpected challenges and disappointments. Thank You for working in Joseph's life in an amazing way. You had a perfect plan for Him even when You carried Him through absolutely awful situations. You worked in Him in such a way that even as a prisoner, He could rise to take care of everything in Potiphar's home. All that Joseph did became a success. You worked through Joseph to create that success. You poured out Your favor on Him. Could You please work in me? Could You please help me succeed in the things I do? Whether I'm working for myself or someone else, could You please pour out Your favor on me? As You do, I want to give You the credit and glory because You are a good, good God, and I trust You. In Your name I ask these things. Amen.

Comforted

Praise be to the God and Father of our Lord Jesus Christ, the Father of compassion and the God of all comfort, who comforts us in all our troubles, so that we can comfort those in any trouble with the comfort we ourselves receive from God.
2 CORINTHIANS 1:3–4 NIV

God of all comfort, I praise You! I praise You because You are good. You're filled with compassion for me and for everyone on earth. You created a beautiful world where we live. I praise You! You created all people, and You know everyone completely. I praise You! And You didn't just create me, but You are near to me. Thank You! You comfort me whenever I'm feeling down or I'm facing any trouble. Even if I don't always remember that You care as much as You do, it doesn't mean You ever stop caring. Your concern and compassion for me never stop, whether I realize it or not. Please help me use Your comfort to help others. Please help me act as Your hands, feet, and voice in this world. I praise You! Amen.

Help Me!

In my distress I called to the LORD; I cried to
my God for help. From his temple he heard my
voice; my cry came before him, into his ears.
PSALM 18:6 NIV

Lord God, help! I feel so helpless and alone right now. I feel like everything is out of my control, and I don't know what will happen. Please help me truly rest in the fact that even if I don't know what's going on, You do. Even if I'm out of control, You're in complete control. Thank You that I can tell You every single detail of my situation and every single concern I have, no matter how big or small it might seem. As I pour out my heart to You, I rest in the truth that You hear my prayers. You listen to my cry for help. And as I cry and pray and beg You for help, You hear and know and will respond. I trust You completely. Please fill me with Your peace as I wait to see the amazing ways You'll help me. In Jesus' name I pray. Amen.

Stop Worrying

"Do not worry about your life, what you will eat or drink; or about your body, what you will wear. Is not life more than food, and the body more than clothes?"

MATTHEW 6:25 NIV

Oh Father, I admit it's easy to worry about a lot of things. It's easy to worry about what will happen next in my life. I can obsess over every little detail, whether it involves my family or friends or school or my future. Lots of other little details are easy to worry about too. Please help me remember Your big picture though. My life is more than the food I eat—and boy, do I like my favorite foods! My life is more than the clothes I wear or what I look like. I don't have to worry about those things or anything else. I can trust You completely. My life is in Your hands. Please help me look to You when I'm tempted to focus on all that's going on around me. I want to kiss my worries goodbye and focus on what's real—not what might or might not happen. In Jesus' name I pray. Amen.

Good Things

*For the LORD God is a sun and shield; the LORD
gives grace and glory; He withholds no good
thing from those who walk with integrity. LORD of
armies, blessed is the person who trusts in You!*

PSALM 84:11-12 NASB

Lord God, You are worthy of my praise and thanks. You
do many amazing things for me and give me so much. You
protect me in ways I'll never realize. You give me plenty
of grace I don't deserve. And You won't ever hold back
good things from me. As long as I walk with You through
my life and live with integrity and complete trust in You,
You'll bless me with every good thing. How wonderful! I
trust in You and want to continue trusting in You all my
life. When I'm tempted to get sidetracked or persuaded
by something or someone else, keep my eyes on You,
Keep my heart fixed on You too! I want to stay close to
You because You are my sun. You're my shield. I'm blessed
when I trust in You. Amen.

Follow the Leader

"I have seen his ways and will heal him.
I will lead him and give comfort to him
and to those who have sorrow for him."

ISAIAH 57:18 NLV

Heavenly Father, Your love and kindness for me truly are amazing. When I worship You and want to follow You with my whole heart and my whole life, You lead me. I may not know what's coming, but You make my every step certain. You keep my path straight even when I have no idea what's coming next. Because of You, I don't have to fear. Plus, You comfort me in amazing ways. Focusing on all that I can see or even all that I can imagine can be tempting. Sometimes my imagination is pretty wonderful and I can picture a future where everything works out for me. But then reality seems a lot more difficult. I get frustrated easily, and it's hard to go through challenging times. Yet every single day You're with me. Please help me follow You when You lead me! In Jesus' name I pray. Amen.

Distracted

*Martha was working hard getting the supper ready.
She came to Jesus and said, "Do You see that my
sister is not helping me? Tell her to help me." Jesus
said to her, "Martha, Martha, you are worried and
troubled about many things. Only a few things
are important, even just one. Mary has chosen the
good thing. It will not be taken away from her."*
LUKE 10:40–42 NLV

Lord God, it's easy for me to get distracted. I have so many
things to do! Whether it's schoolwork or chores or activ-
ities or spending time with my family and friends, when I
focus on what I need to do, I often stress. I get distracted
by other people and what they are doing or aren't doing.
Instead of focusing so much on other people or keeping
busy, please help me find time just to be with You. I want
to spend more time with You. Please help me find a way
to be still and know You're God. I want to communicate
with You by praying more often. And I want to get to know
who You are through Your Word. Please help me lose my
focus on worldly things and create a focus on You! In Your
name I pray. Amen.

Living in Truth

"These are the things which you shall do: speak the truth to one another; judge with truth and judgment for peace at your gates."

ZECHARIAH 8:16 NASB

Father, sometimes I like to know what I should or shouldn't do. It's a little easier to know what's expected. I'm thankful the Bible gives me details of what You'd like my life to look like. When You ask me to live an honest life, I know that lying and deceitfulness are exactly what I need to avoid. When I'm tempted to stretch the truth, please help me choose honesty instead. When it seems like a lie would be an easier way to cover up something that's difficult or uncomfortable to say, please help me to be truthful! I need to speak the truth. And I need to judge with truth. Even when it's difficult and even when I'm tempted to make an easier, dishonest choice, please help me choose what's right and true. As I do, please help me experience Your peace. In Jesus' name I pray. Amen.

The Comparison Trap

We do not dare to classify or compare ourselves with some who commend themselves. When they measure themselves by themselves and compare themselves with themselves, they are not wise.

2 CORINTHIANS 10:12 NIV

Father, sometimes when I see what other people are doing or what they have, I start comparing what I can do or what I have. Whether I think I'm better than someone else or simply not good enough, it's like I'm measuring myself on a scale that's constantly moving. Please help me stop doing this! I don't want to compare myself with others. Please help me remember that You've created every single person to be unique. We all have different strengths and weaknesses, and You have a completely different plan for every single life. Please help me to be grateful for the life You've given me and help me use my gifts for You. I want to be the best *me* possible, and I can't do that if I'm constantly trying to copy or be better than other people. In Jesus' name I pray. Amen.

Peace and Safety

I will lie down and sleep in peace.
O Lord, You alone keep me safe.
PSALM 4:8 NLV

O Lord, You keep me safe more than anything else in this world. As much as I might try to find my peace or security in other things or people, You alone are the One who floods my heart with peace. You alone are the One who keeps me safe. Thank You! When I lie down tonight, please help me remember this truth. I want to give You all the cares of my day, thank You for everything good that's happened, and truly rest in You. I don't have to worry about anything that's happened in my day or anything that might happen tomorrow. Everything is under Your control. I can rest in Your power and Your good plan. Thank You for protecting me, and thank You for Your good, comforting gift of peace! In Jesus' name I pray. Amen.

A Strong Guide

*"In your unfailing love you will lead the people
you have redeemed. In your strength you
will guide them to your holy dwelling."*
EXODUS 15:13 NIV

Father, all throughout the Bible You've given examples of the ways You've taken care of people You've chosen. In the Old Testament, You led the Israelites in a mighty and miraculous way. And in the New Testament, You faithfully guided and worked through people who trusted in You completely. When I consider all You've done for people You call Your own, I'm in awe. I'm in awe of the way You provide every single need. I'm in awe of the way You work situations for good for those who know and love You. And I'm in awe of the way You lovingly and patiently guide. None of this is half-hearted on Your part. You do everything with Your holy strength and might. I want You to guide me too! Please lead me with Your unfailing love. I love You and trust You! In Jesus' name I pray. Amen.

Complete Rest

God's people have a complete rest waiting for them.
The man who goes into God's rest, rests from his
own work the same as God rested from His work.
HEBREWS 4:9–10 NLV

Father God, You created all things. I'm in awe over the fact that You could do absolutely anything. You created the entire world and everything in it in six days! It was good. Then You rested. As the God of the universe, I'm sure You didn't need to rest, but You did as an example for me. And through Your gift of Jesus, I have complete rest for my soul. When I believe in Him, I suddenly gain access to Your rest. I don't have to work to try to save myself. I don't have to do more or try to be more. In all my weakness and failings, You offer forgiveness. Thank You for offering me Your good rest. I'll happily take it! I pray that as I do, I'll stop trying to work so hard for Your love and approval. Please help me remember that You love me, and that You started loving me even before I was born. In Jesus' name I pray. Amen.

A Much-Needed Rescue

Rescue me from my enemies, my God; set me securely on high away from those who rise up against me. Rescue me from those who practice injustice, and save me from men of bloodshed.
PSALM 59:1-2 NASB

Lord, You know the way enemies abound in this world. And You know who my enemies are, even if I don't. I pray that You'll rescue me. Please keep me safe from evil plans. Please protect me from any plots that are meant to harm me. I pray You'll confuse and bring to light any plans of the wicked. I get so frustrated and angry when evil people prosper. Please help me remember that You're the ultimate Judge, and You see and know exactly what people do. Help me to take comfort in the fact that You will punish evil in Your time. For now, I want to run to You. When I get scared, please comfort me and remind me that You're my strong, safe place. Please protect and rescue me. I'm depending on You! In Your holy name I pray. Amen.

The Right Words at the Right Time

"When you are put into their hands, do not worry what you will say or how you will say it. The words will be given you when the time comes."
MATTHEW 10:19 NLV

Father, it's easy to worry when I wonder what will happen to me in this life. Will evil people prosper? Will I be persecuted for my faith in You? When I have so many ideas and questions, please help me remember that You are the ultimate answer. And as I trust in You completely, You'll give me the exact words to say at the right time. I don't have to fear. I don't have to plan what I'll say or do. All I need is to trust You. Please give me peace as I wait for You. And please fill my mouth with the right words. Speak through me. Use my mouth and my voice to speak Your truth into this world. I love You and want to rest in the peace that only You can bring. Thank You for being completely worthy of my trust. I love You!

Greater Than I Realize

I looked for the Lord, and He answered
me. And He took away all my fears.
PSALM 34:4 NLV

Lord, You promise in Your Word that when I look for You, I'll find You. When I call to You, You'll answer me. When I'm scared, You'll take away all my fears. You're always there, always listening, and always ready to help me. You are so much greater and kinder than I realize. Unfortunately, I don't always make the most of Your faithfulness and love. Some days I forget about You. I get busy and sidetracked. I don't always look for You. I don't talk to You or listen for You as much as I'd like. And sometimes I'd rather dwell on my worries and fears instead of totally placing my trust in You. Please help me turn to You more and more every day. I want to get closer to You! In Jesus' name I pray. Amen.

Gladness and Joy

"Then young women will dance and be glad, young men and old as well. I will turn their mourning into gladness; I will give them comfort and joy instead of sorrow."

JEREMIAH 31:13 NIV

Father, life isn't easy. You never promised it would be, but when I need to face challenges and hard times, it's easy to get discouraged. In my times of frustration and disappointment, I want to turn to You. When I do, You'll change my perspective. When I trust You in hard times, You'll give me peace and comfort I could never create on my own. Just as the prophet Jeremiah promised the Israelites, You will turn mourning into gladness. You'll replace sorrow with comfort and joy. You have the power to do that, and Lord, I pray You'll do it in my life! Please turn my sorrows to joy! Please turn my mourning into gladness. Please right the wrongs in my life. I'm so thankful You're my God, and I trust You completely. In Jesus' name I pray. Amen.

Filled to Overflowing

The fruit of the Spirit is love, joy, peace, patience,
kindness, goodness, faithfulness, gentleness,
self-control; against such things there is no law.
GALATIANS 5:22–23 NASB

Lord God, I praise You for the way You work in my life. I praise You for the gift of Your Holy Spirit. When I come to know You, You fill me with Your Spirit, and as I walk closely with Him moment by moment, He can't help but spill out of me in a wonderful way. It's like I start bearing all of this really good fruit I could never create on my own. Through Your Spirit, You give me true love and joy that overflows to others. Your peace comforts me in an amazing way. I grow in patience, both with myself and with others. You give me the ability to treat others with kindness and gentleness. Because of You, I can be faithful and good. And You help me control myself. Thank You! I'm so grateful You let me experience all of Your good gifts then let them overflow out of me to others. Please use me to bless others! In Jesus' name I pray. Amen.

The Offer of Peace

"You will keep the man in perfect peace whose mind is kept on You, because he trusts in You."

ISAIAH 26:3 NLV

Father God, Your peace is something I can't quite understand, but I definitely can experience it! And when I do, I'm amazed. I don't have to fear anything in this life, and I don't have to worry. The thing is, while You're more than willing and able to give me Your peace, it doesn't just come to me automatically. I have to trust in You. And I have to keep my mind on You. When I trust in myself and keep my mind focused on my own thoughts and concerns, peace disappears and my worries start multiplying. But when I turn my focus to You, Your peace starts to flood my heart and mind. When I keep my mind on You, You fill me with Your unmistakable, unshakable peace. Deep down I want to keep my mind on You all the time. Please help me think of You and trust in You even when this world tries to pull my thoughts away. In Jesus' holy name I pray. Amen.

Doing What You'd Have Done

"Do not judge, and you will not be judged. Do not condemn, and you will not be condemned. Forgive, and you will be forgiven."

LUKE 6:37 NIV

Lord, many days it's easy to forget about what other people might be going through. It's easy to forget to treat people the way I'd like to be treated. Please help me remember to do this! When I'm tempted to look at what someone else is saying or doing and judge them, I want to stop. I don't want people to judge me, so I shouldn't judge them either. When I'm tempted to condemn someone else for any reason, please stop me from doing it. I don't want anyone to condemn me, and I have no right to condemn someone else. When I'm tempted to hold on to a grudge and be unforgiving, please help me to forgive. And when I mess up or hurt someone else, I want to be forgiven. In the same way, help me forgive others too. Just as You've shown me so much grace I don't deserve, please help me to be more like You and treat others with grace. Amen.

Don't Turn Back

I will hear what God the LORD will say; for He will
speak peace to His people, to His godly ones;
and may they not turn back to foolishness.
PSALM 85:8 NASB

Lord God, thank You for the way You speak peace to Your people. Because You're the Lord of the universe, You could say absolutely anything to anyone. Yet You choose Your own people, and You choose to speak peace. You do this in a loving and gentle way so Your chosen ones won't turn back to foolishness. Since You've called me to Yourself and I've responded to You, please help me accept Your peace and Your wise way of living. I don't want to turn back to foolishness! I want to honor and please You in all that I say and do. In the moments that I mess up and forget that I'm Your daughter, please forgive me. Then help me turn back to say and do what is right in Your sight. I love You, and I'm thankful for all You've done for me. In Jesus' name I pray. Amen.

Pointing Others to Jesus

"For the despairing man there should be kindness from his friend; so that he does not abandon the fear of the Almighty."

JOB 6:14 NASB

Almighty God, the way I treat other people reflects my love and respect for You. I could treat others absolutely any way I feel like treating them. I could be mean and nasty. I could be harsh and judgmental. I could ignore them. Or I could be caring and concerned. I could be gentle and try to make peace. I could be kind and loving. If I choose to treat others with the sort of love and kindness that You've shown me, I demonstrate to the world that I have a healthy fear of and respect for You. When I treat other people with Your kindness and grace, I help anyone in despair begin to fear and respect You too. I can point others to Jesus by the way I treat them. Please help me remember and live in light of this! In Jesus' name I pray. Amen.

True Beauty

*Your beauty should come from the inside.
It should come from the heart. This is the
kind that lasts. Your beauty should be a gentle
and quiet spirit. In God's sight this is of great
worth and no amount of money can buy it.*

1 PETER 3:4 NLV

Heavenly Father, so very much in this world focuses on outward appearances. It's hard not to get sucked into the temptation to focus on what other people look like—or what I look like. What people look like truly doesn't matter. Please help me look beyond appearances to see who people really are. And please help me focus on making my own character and personality beautiful. You know my heart, and You know if it's beautiful or not. Some kind of tragedy could cause my looks to change in a split second, but my heart will endure. If my inner spirit is ugly, please root out the flaws. Open my eyes to see an accurate picture of my character, and help my spirit to become beautiful. Please give my heart a makeover! Amen.

Worthy of Praise

I called to the LORD, who is worthy of praise,
and I have been saved from my enemies.
PSALM 18:3 NIV

Lord, I praise You! You are so much more amazing than I realize. I want to stop and think about the way You've worked in this world. You created everything! You have a plan for every person. Absolutely nothing escapes Your notice. You are always present. You always know everything. Nothing comes as a surprise to You. You know me completely, and You still love me. Thank You! You listen to me when I call out to You. When my enemies seek to harm me or create bad situations in my life, You save me. Because of You and Your protection and care, I don't have to fear. You're worthy of my trust, and You're worthy of my praise. You are a good, good God, and I'm so thankful You've called me to be part of Your family. In Jesus' name I pray. Amen.

What's Ruling Your Heart?

*Let the peace of Christ rule in your hearts,
since as members of one body you were
called to peace. And be thankful.*
COLOSSIANS 3:15 NIV

Lord God, every day I choose what will rule my heart. Will my own feelings take control? Will I be led by my emotions and desires? Will I practice self-control? Even if I feel like I'm not making a choice and just going with the flow, that's still a decision. Please help me to be more mindful of what I'm doing and saying. Open my eyes to how my thoughts affect my behavior and attitude. Instead of reacting to situations, show me how I have the freedom to respond. It's so easy to feel like I have the right to say or do whatever I please. Deep down though, I know that kind of life isn't necessarily Your best for me. Please help the peace of Christ rule in my heart. When I'm tempted to react to situations out of fear or worry, help His peace wash over me. I can fully rest in You, no matter what. Thank You for that good gift! I want to live in Your rest and Your peace! In Jesus' name I pray. Amen.

Loyalty or Lies?

They remembered that God was their Rock, that God Most High was their Redeemer. But then they would flatter him with their mouths, lying to him with their tongues; their hearts were not loyal to him, they were not faithful to his covenant.
PSALM 78:35–37 NIV

Oh Lord, how many times have Your chosen people worshipped You and then turned away? The Bible tells of many people who honored You with their mouths but dishonored You with their hearts. I don't want that to be true of me, Father! I love You! I want to faithfully honor and obey You. You are my Rock. You've rescued my life from the punishment of sin. I want to be loyal to You! I want to faithfully keep any promises I've made to You. I don't want to be fickle and forever change my mind. I want to be devoted to You. You don't need my flattery or praise. You don't want a bunch of empty words. And I don't want to be known as a liar. I don't want to turn away from You and go my own way. Lord, my sincere desire is to be faithful to You! Please help me stand up against temptations in this life. I want to loyally and consistently love and worship You. In Jesus' name I pray. Amen.

Do Not Be Afraid

"Do not fear, for I am with you. Do not be afraid, for I am your God. I will give you strength, and for sure I will help you. Yes, I will hold you up with My right hand that is right and good."

ISAIAH 41:10 NLV

Father God, there's a lot to be scared of in this world. I can try to be brave on my own, but I can only do so much. You, however, can do amazing things! Because of You and Your strength and power, I don't have to fear. You're always, always with me! You are my heavenly Father, and I am Your child. You'll protect me and help me. You'll give me strength even when I feel weak. You'll hold me up when I stumble and fall. I want to remember all the good things You do for me, so that when I'm in the middle of a situation and I'm afraid or worried or nervous, I'll be comforted by You and Your truth. Thank You for giving me a reason and the strength to be brave. Thank You for working through me in amazing ways. Thank You for Your help and loving care. You are such a good, good God! In Jesus' name I pray. Amen.

Living Like I'm Chosen

As God's chosen people, holy and dearly loved,
clothe yourselves with compassion, kindness,
humility, gentleness and patience.
COLOSSIANS 3:12 NIV

Lord, when I stop to consider that You've chosen me, I'm amazed. I didn't have to do anything for Your favor, but You've poured it out on me in so many ways. You love me dearly, and You even consider me to be holy. Those facts are more than I can fully comprehend. Even if I don't understand how or why I'm so special to You, I can believe it! Because I'm Yours, I want to live like it. I want my thoughts, actions, words, and choices to reflect my love and devotion to You. Please help me to be compassionate and kind to everyone—my friends, enemies, and everyone else! I don't want to be puffed up with pride. Please help me to humbly remember who I am and to be gentle. And please help my patience to grow even when I may not enjoy it. I love You and want my life to mirror You. In Jesus' name I pray. Amen.

Make Plans for Peace

*Lying is in the heart of those who plan what
is bad, but those who plan peace have joy.*
PROVERBS 12:20 NLV

Father, whether I realize it or not, all day long I make choices that reveal my heart and my intentions. I can choose wrong and try to get back at people or act out in frustration, anger, and annoyance. Or I can choose right and look for ways to make someone else's life better. Could You please help me choose what's right and strengthen me to do what's right in Your eyes? I don't want to plan bad things. I want to do good, even when I don't feel like it. I don't want to become a liar. I want to be honest even when it's uncomfortable. Please help me plan peaceful, good things. I'd love to add peace to this world just because I'm Your daughter. Knowing You will give me joy is an added bonus. Thank You! I'm so glad I can be Your representative wherever I live. I Jesus' name I pray. Amen.

More Than What You See

*"Do not judge by the outward appearance,
but judge with righteous judgment."*
JOHN 7:24 NASB

Oh Lord, I confess that so many times I judge people or situations based on appearances. I don't try to find out details, and I don't stop to consider what someone else might be experiencing. I need to stop doing that! You look beyond the surface and see what's in the heart. You know what's happening behind the scenes. I'm not You though, and I'll never be able to have Your unlimited wisdom. But I can try to be more like You every day. And when it comes to my thoughts and reactions toward people, I can stop and try to get a better picture of what might be going on. I can try to judge rightly and discern justly. Please open my eyes to the truth and to see situations and people with Your perspective. In Jesus' name I pray. Amen.

Choosing Pride or Humility

*The meek will inherit the land and
enjoy peace and prosperity.*
PSALM 37:11 NIV

Father, so much of this world is focused on pride. It's easy to puff myself up so others can think of me a certain way. I don't mind bragging or making my life appear better than it really is. I can focus so much on myself and what I think is good about me that I start to get puffed up. I can focus on my appearance or my talents or possessions. That's not Your way though! If anyone has a reason to brag or be proud, it's You. The rest of creation can't even begin to compare to how great You are. Compared to You, I'm so tiny. I want to consider You and Your majestic greatness. When I do, I can praise You for who You are and keep a right perspective of who I am. Compared to You, I should feel humbled. I want to be gentle and kind instead of arrogant and selfish. You oppose the proud, and I don't want You to oppose me! As I choose a meek and humble way of thinking and living, You've promised to bless me with peace and prosperity. Thank You for those good gifts. Please help me humbly remember who I am and who You are. In Jesus' name I pray. Amen.

Becoming a Good Friend

A friend loves at all times.
A brother is born to share troubles.
PROVERBS 17:17 NLV

Lord God, You've blessed me with friendships that fill my life with happiness and laughter. I'm so thankful for my good friends! I pray that I will be a good friend to my friends. I want to become the kind of friend I'd like to have. Please help me to be loving and thoughtful. Even when it might seem uncomfortable, I want to share my friends' troubles by being caring and a good listener. Help me speak Your truth to my friends in a gentle, loving way. If my friends need help that's beyond something I can offer, could You please guide me in the right direction? I want to love and be a trustworthy confidante, but I also know I can't always shoulder all of my friends' burdens on my own. Please fill me with Your wisdom and help me to be a good, good friend. In Jesus' name I pray. Amen.

Strength in Weakness

He said to me, "My grace is sufficient for you, for my power is made perfect in weakness." Therefore I will boast all the more gladly about my weaknesses, so that Christ's power may rest on me.

2 CORINTHIANS 12:9 NIV

Father, because I'm feeling pretty weak right now, it's such a huge relief to know that Your power is perfected in weakness! I know I can't do everything on my own. I don't have enough ideas or inspiration. I doubt I have enough strength or energy or courage. I want You to use me in any way, but I admit that I feel like I don't have so much to offer. Please work through me, Lord, just as You've promised. I'm thankful Your grace is all I need. I trust You to work in me and through me. Use my weaknesses in any way and help me do amazing things through You and Your power. I love You, and I'm so grateful You never expect perfection from me. Instead, You let me be myself, and then You perform great works. Thank You! In Jesus' name I pray. Amen.

Where's Your Trust?

In you, LORD my God, I put my trust.
I trust in you; do not let me be put to shame,
nor let my enemies triumph over me.

PSALM 25:1–2 NIV

Lord my God, I admit I don't always trust You completely. Sometimes I doubt Your way for me is the best way. Other times I try to take matters into my own hands and trust myself. That's just foolishness though! Who am I to trust in myself when I know all my weaknesses and imperfections? But when I put my trust in You, everything changes. You're almighty God. You're all-powerful. You're all-knowing. You're worthy of my praise and my trust. I can put my trust in You, knowing You won't let me be put to shame. You'll protect me and lead the way. As I follow You, You'll guide me into good places. I can take comfort and rest in You, and for that I'm grateful. Thank You! I love You!

Filled with Good Things

May the God of hope fill you with all joy and peace
as you trust in him, so that you may overflow
with hope by the power of the Holy Spirit.
ROMANS 15:13 NIV

Father, You have a wonderful way of heaping goodness into my life. If I stop and think about all the good things You do for me, whether they're big or little, I'm thankful! And when I trust in You more and more, You give me even better gifts. You are the God of hope. I can believe in You and expect You to work in my life. I can trust that You'll fill me with all joy and all peace—not just a little. And as You bless me with joy and peace, I'll be filled to overflowing with hope in You. Thank You for being a God who loves to pour out Your goodness until it all overflows in my life. Please help me share Your joy and peace and hope with people around me, through the power of the Holy Spirit. Thank You for the way You lavish Your love and kindness on me! In Jesus' name I pray. Amen.

Being Near God

*As for me, it is good to be near God. I have
made the Lord God my safe place. So I may
tell of all the things You have done.*

PSALM 73:28 NLV

Lord God, You are a safe place in a dangerous world. I can trust in You completely, and You'll keep me safe and secure. But I need to come to You instead of taking for granted that You're always there for me. When I choose to come near to You, You'll come near to me. And since it's such a good thing to be near You, I pray that I might get closer and closer. As I get nearer to You and get to know You better, I'll be able to clearly see so many of the things You've done in my life and in the world around me. I see You at work, and I praise You for the mighty way You lovingly protect Your chosen ones. Thank You for all that You do for me. Please soften my heart and help me make time and space to get nearer to You. In Jesus' holy name I pray. Amen.

Helped!

"I am the LORD your God who takes hold of your right hand, Who says to you, 'Do not fear, I will help you.'"
ISAIAH 41:13 NASB

Father, it's such a huge comfort to know that You take me by the hand and never leave me. You help me. And because of You, I don't have to fear. I also don't have to feel lonely, because You're always there for me. Thank You! I want to rest in You and Your loving, caring protection for me. I admit I definitely need Your help! In fact, sometimes I feel pretty helpless and afraid, so knowing that You're there for me is a huge relief. Please help me to trust You more and more and to relax. I'm so thankful that because You are in control, I don't have to live a life full of worry or fear. Please open my eyes so I can see all the different ways You help me. I want to know that good things that happen aren't a coincidence but are good gifts from You. In Jesus' name I pray. Amen.

Not Caving In

*Even if you suffer for doing what is right, you
will be happy. Do not be afraid or troubled by
what they may do to make it hard for you.*

1 PETER 3:14 NLV

Almighty God, I praise You for Your righteousness and
holiness. You are perfect in Your goodness and kindness.
I want to be like You even when that feels really challenging. Please fill me with Your Spirit and guide me to make
the right choices. No matter what the world might say—
whether I'm getting messages or demands from leaders
or my friends or family members—help me stand strong
and not cave in to pressure. When something is right, I
want to do it. And if something is wrong, I want to stand
for my beliefs and not give in. Even if I end up suffering
from doing what is right, please help me follow through.
I don't want to live in fear of what others think or might
do to me. I want to focus on You and live a life that's holy
and pleasing to You. Please give me the strength to do
that, Lord. In Jesus' name I pray. Amen.

Trusting the God of Miracles

The LORD gave them rest on every side, in accordance with everything that He had sworn to their fathers, and no one of all their enemies stood before them; the LORD handed all their enemies over to them.
JOSHUA 21:44 NASB

Lord God, You are good. You always keep Your promises, and You always protect Your people. I'm thankful for examples of Your faithfulness in the Bible. Please remind me that You're the same God today as You were in Bible times, and You're as faithful today as You've ever been. Thank You for Your good gift of rest. Even when I feel like I'm in the middle of a battle or my enemies are intimidating, I can trust You to work all things out for good. I love You and I trust You. I can hardly wait to see the ways You'll work in my life. I want to trust You more and more every day. I don't have to base my life and decisions on my feelings. Instead, I can live with absolute confidence in my faith in You. You're the God of miracles, and I worship You. In Jesus' name I pray. Amen.

You Do You

Jesus said, "If I want this one to wait until I come, what is that to you? You follow Me."
JOHN 21:22 NLV

Father, You know my tendency is to compare myself with other people or even what I think I should be like. How often do I get sidetracked by focusing on something I really don't need to consider? What I really wish I could do is focus on Your will and plan for my life. You've gifted me in a specific, unique way. I'm not like anyone else. And You have very specific, unique plans and purposes for my life. Please help me live my life like a track star and stay in my own lane. I don't want to trip over what other runners are doing or focus on how fast they're moving. Instead, please help me run the race You've set up for me. I know You're doing lots of other things in everyone else's lives—that's what You do! But what is it to me if You choose different stories and twists and turns for every single person? Help me focus on You alone and follow You with my whole heart. Thank You for my life's unique adventure! In Jesus' name I pray. Amen.

He Loves Me Anyway

*The LORD looks down from heaven on the
children of man, to see if there are any
who understand, who seek after God.*
PSALM 14:2 ESV

Lord, I know You see all things and know all things. You search human hearts and know what's truly inside, including every person's thoughts. When it comes to You, I don't have to try to pretend I'm someone I'm not, because You know me completely. I'm sorry for the ways I mess up over and over again. You know if and when I seek after You and if and when I seek after myself. Lord, I want to focus more on You and less on myself. I know this won't happen overnight. In fact, it's something I'll deal with my entire life. But I love You and want to be devoted to You. I'm thankful that You're patient and understanding. You know my strengths and weaknesses. You know my limitations, and You love me anyway. Thank You! I love You! In Jesus' name I pray. Amen.

Treasured

*He said, "You who are treasured, do not be
afraid. Peace be to you; take courage and be
courageous!" Now as soon as he spoke to me,
I felt strengthened and said, "May my lord
speak, for you have strengthened me."*

DANIEL 10:19 NASB

Oh Lord, to know that You treasure Your loved ones is
such an amazing comfort. It's beautiful to my ears. Thank
You for treasuring me. It's also a comfort to know that I
don't have to be afraid. I don't have to live in fear, because
You are the all-powerful God. You give courage, and You
walk with those You love. Please help me in my fear and
doubting. When I feel afraid, I want to take courage in
You alone. I don't want to live in fear anymore. Strengthen
me in a way that only You can. I'm so thankful that in You
I can be strong and courageous. I want to step out in
faith, knowing that You will guide and protect me. You will
give me peace. Thank You! In Jesus' name I pray. Amen.

Follow His Way

*"Follow My teachings and learn from Me. I am gentle
and do not have pride. You will have rest for your souls."*
MATTHEW 11:29 NLV

Jesus, thank You for coming to earth to offer what no
human could earn or achieve on their own. You offer me
forever life with You if and when I believe in You. But
instead of only giving something for eternity, You also
offer a great gift of rest right now. And not just a rest
like I'm feeling relaxed right now, but a deep, soul rest.
The way You gently offer it is so caring, but this kind of
invitation also means I need to respond. I can choose to
take Your rest. I can choose to learn from You and follow
Your teachings. Or I can choose to ignore Your offer
or push it to the side until I feel like I'm prepared. You
never said I need to get my act together first though.
You never said I need to come to You if I do a certain
amount of chores or get my heart just right. You only tell
me to follow Your teachings. I want to drop everything
that stands in the way, Lord, and learn from You. I want
to follow You. In Your name I pray. Amen.

Thinking before Doing

Ponder the path of your feet; then
all your ways will be sure.
PROVERBS 4:26 ESV

Father God, when You created humans, You never intended for us just to float along in life, reacting to whatever circumstances happen. While that certainly is one way to approach life, in Your Word You've taught that choices make a huge difference. When I watch the way I'm going, I'll have a better life. When I choose right living, I'll grow closer to You and see so much good. It can be hard to think through the things I do every day though. It's easier to try to go with the flow. When I'm tempted to take the easy way and do whatever feels natural or what others pressure me to do, please prick my conscience. Remind me that I have a choice in what I do and the way I respond to everything. Please help me know what's right and wrong. Please help me think through the good and bad outcomes of my choices. I want to watch the path of my feet so my ways will be sure. Thank You for Your help and Your wisdom. And thank You for the truth of the Word and the way it guides me! In Jesus' name I pray. Amen.

Who's the Boss?

*If your sinful old self is the boss over your mind,
it leads to death. But if the Holy Spirit is the boss
over your mind, it leads to life and peace.*

ROMANS 8:6 NLV

Lord, You've been so good to offer me life instead of death. You offer me peace instead of doubt and despair. All of the good doesn't instantly and naturally come to me though. It's all based on my decisions. I can choose life and peace. Or I can choose fear and doubt and death. If I want to choose peace—and I do!—I need to be willing to let the Holy Spirit lead me. He needs to become my boss. I need not only to listen to Him, but also to obey Him. If I choose to sin over and over again because it seems fun or feels good, I'll become numb to what I'm doing wrong and deaf to the quiet way the Spirit speaks to me. I don't want to drown out His voice with a bunch of sin! Please help me make the hard choices to stay away from sin. I want to follow You and Your right, life-giving way. In Jesus' name I pray. Amen.

Frustrated with Frustration

My soul is in deep anguish. How long, LORD, how long?
PSALM 6:3 NIV

Oh Lord, when I'm going through hard times, it feels like my struggles and challenges will go on forever. I don't feel right, and I can't stop thinking about my difficulties. It's so frustrating! I'm not being overly dramatic when I tell You that I feel like I'm in anguish. Could You please help me? Could You please bring an end to all of my discouragement? I wish everything could be better right now. Or if things can't be completely resolved, I wish You could at least show me the way my situation is improving. But sometimes I just need to learn to wait for You through all the ugliness. I need to learn to trust You and be patient. I need to keep hoping that You'll make all things right. Endurance isn't easy, but it will make me a better person in the long run. Until then, I pray You'll help me patiently endure while I suffer. I pray for Your mercy as I feel miserable. And I pray I'll experience Your love in new and real ways every day. In Jesus' holy name I pray. Amen.

Paying Attention

"Oh that you had paid attention to my commandments!
Then your peace would have been like a river, and
your righteousness like the waves of the sea."
ISAIAH 48:18 ESV

Lord, You are so good and generous to offer me peace. You offer not just a moment of peace, but ongoing peace that flows like a river, steady and strong. And You promise me right living that keeps coming and coming, as constant and sure as the waves of the sea. Thank You! Your offer is conditional though. I need to respond so that I can experience Your peace and righteousness. I need to pay attention to Your commands. To pay attention to them, I need to know them. Because of that, please help me find moments in my day when I can read the Bible more often. I may not always have a lot of time to read and study it, but in the moments that I can, please help me really think about what is written. May Your Word impact my heart and mind so that I make good choices. I want to pay attention to Your commands! And I want Your good gifts of peace and righteousness. I love You, and I'm grateful for the ways You fill my life with amazing blessings. In Jesus' name I pray. Amen.

Questions and Answers

Jesus said to them, "Why are you afraid?
Why do you have doubts in your hearts?"
LUKE 24:38 NLV

Jesus, when You lived on this earth, You knew exactly what was in people's hearts. You understood what they wrestled with, thought, and felt. And the great thing is, You helped people deal with their thoughts and feelings. You didn't preach bossy, critical messages that made people feel bad about themselves, but You asked questions. Your questions cut right to the heart of the matter. When Your disciples were afraid, You didn't scold them for their fear, but You did ask why they were afraid. You knew that fear is directly tied to doubt, but again, You didn't criticize the doubts. You simply asked why they had doubts in their hearts. If You were here today, Lord, You could ask me the same questions. Why am I afraid? Why do I have doubts in my heart? I want to think these questions over and surrender my fear and doubt to You. In Your name I pray. Amen.

Peace and Rest

"You will have a son who will be a man of peace and rest, and I will give him rest from all his enemies on every side. His name will be Solomon, and I will grant Israel peace and quiet during his reign."

1 CHRONICLES 22:9 NIV

Lord, Your Word describes the way You give peace and rest. In the Old Testament, You promised David that His son, Solomon, would be a man of peace and rest. And when Solomon reigned as king, You gave Israel peace and rest. Just as You give peace and rest as a great gift, You also allow conflict and disagreements. I pray that You'll guard me and keep me from trouble. Please help me become a peacemaker. Help me listen to both sides of a story and help others keep the peace. Instead of picking a fight or always looking for a reason to disagree or complain, I'd love to find the good in a person or situation. Please help me smooth rough situations over with my family and friends. Even when it's difficult or uncomfortable, I want to work for peace. Could You please help me? I love You, I trust You, and I want to be Your representative in this stress-filled world. In Jesus' name I ask all these things. Amen.

Harvesting What You Plant

*Those who plant seeds of peace will
gather what is right and good.*
JAMES 3:18 NLV

Father, being peaceful or trying to make peace in this world really isn't that easy. In fact, when I try to avoid a conflict or break up a fight, peace seems almost impossible—especially if others oppose me. While You never said that keeping peace was easy, Your Word does teach that a lot of good comes out of it. If I plant seeds of peace, I'll gather a right and good harvest. My attitude and words plant seeds anyway. Since everything I do could be seen as a seed, why not just plant goodness? If I plant a crop of nastiness, cruelty, sarcasm, anger, disgust, or hatred, I'll harvest something pretty awful. But when I plant peace, kindness, gentleness, joy, patience, or love, my harvest will be right and good. Please help me to see the peaceful way and choose to live it! In Jesus' name I pray. Amen.

Living with Liars

They do not speak peaceably, but devise false accusations against those who live quietly in the land.
PSALM 35:20 NIV

Father, I hate it when people lie about me. I just wish everyone would treat me fairly and kindly! But that's just not the way this world works. Even if people falsely accuse me or if they're mean to me for no reason at all, please help me respond in a way that honors You. I pray that my character and reputation would mirror my belief in You, so that even if people do falsely accuse me, they'll be put to shame. I really don't like experiencing conflict. Please teach me something from this! Even if I learn how I don't want to be treated or how I don't want to treat others, those are good lessons that can change my life. Please keep me from repeating rumors or saying outright lies about other people. I don't want to wrongly accuse, and I don't want to fall into the trap of speaking poorly about others. Please help me!

Need Some Advice?

Oil and perfume make the heart glad,
and a person's advice is sweet to his friend.
PROVERBS 27:9 NASB

Lord, sometimes when my friends ask me for advice, I don't exactly know what to say. I don't want to lead them in the wrong direction. And it's hard to think about different sides of a story and needing to think about how I should advise my friend. After all, I want the best for my friends! Please help me remember that my advice doesn't have to be perfectly wise. In fact, I can really help out just by listening to my friend talk. Sometimes people can see their situations clearly once they talk about the details. Help me to be a listening ear. I want to show that I care, even if I'm not exactly sure what kind of advice would be good. Please give me wisdom! Help me see my friend's situation clearly. And please help me to look at things through Your eyes. In Jesus' name I pray. Amen.

Come Away and Rest

*And He said to them, "Come away by yourselves
to a secluded place and rest a little while." (For
there were many people coming and going,
and they did not even have time to eat.)*

MARK 6:31 NASB

Lord Jesus, when You walked on this earth, You knew how important it was to get away from crowds. You got away to pray, and when You and Your disciples were in the middle of a really busy time of life, You invited them to come away and rest a little while. It's so nice to realize that You cared about them so much and knew they needed to rest and recharge—and take time to eat! The same can be true in my life. When I'm busy and constantly surrounded by people and things to do, I get worn out. I need time to get away by myself and rest a little while. I need to take some time out to enjoy a meal. Always running from activity to activity isn't healthy for my body or my soul. Thanks for that reminder. Like Your disciples, I want to come away to a secluded place to spend time resting with You. Please help me make this a reality! In Your name I pray. Amen.

Safely Set on High

"He makes my feet like the feet of a deer.
He sets me safe on high places."
2 SAMUEL 22:34 NLV

Lord, thank You for the many ways You care for me and protect me when I don't even realize it. You set me safe on high places that are out of reach from danger. And You make my feet like the feet of a deer—quick and nimble and able to leap out of harm's way at a moment's notice. If I relied only on myself and my own judgment and ability to stay safe, I think I'd seem more like a sloth—slow and a little unaware of what's really going on. But You are my great protector, and for that I'm very thankful. You don't only protect me physically, but You mentally and spiritually protect me too. You do many loving, kind, and helpful things for me that I don't even see or realize. You care for me in amazing ways. Thank You! I love You!

God's Good Gift of Peace

*The peace of God is much greater than the
human mind can understand. This peace will keep
your hearts and minds through Christ Jesus.*
PHILIPPIANS 4:7 NLV

Lord God, You give an amazing gift of peace. I can't understand the way it makes me feel, but I know it helps me feel calm. You fill my heart with Your peace so I feel hopeful and relaxed as I trust You. And when I let You fill my mind with Your peace, my worries disappear. It's pretty amazing, actually. Experiencing Your peace is a great way for me to tell if I'm truly trusting in You or trying to solve all my own problems and carry my own burdens. When I feel really stressed out and don't experience Your peace, it's a giveaway that I'm focused on the things of this world. Please help me cast all my cares and worries on You! I'll gladly toss them over to You right now. As much as I might like to know details and solutions and how everything will work out, I choose to trust You. As I do, please fill me with Your amazing peace. In Jesus' name I pray. Amen.

So Much Good

Many, LORD my God, are the wonders you have done, the things you planned for us. None can compare with you; were I to speak and tell of your deeds, they would be too many to declare.

PSALM 40:5 NIV

Lord, You are so very good to me! It amazes me to think of all the wonderful things You've done in my life. You've gifted me in many ways. I don't want to brag to anyone else, but I'll thank You that You've given me some pretty great talents! When I think about the people in my life who love and care for me, I'm thankful for the way You use them to make me a better person. And when I consider the different moments in my life when You've done really good things for me, I'm grateful! Even when I get moody or feel tempted to throw a pity party for myself and think that things are difficult, I can't deny the fact that You have filled my life with great gifts. I love the way You know me perfectly, then show Your love for me by working in my life in a wonderful way. Thank You!

Revived

This is what the high and exalted One Who lives forever, whose name is Holy, says: "I dwell in a high and holy place, and also with the contrite and lowly of spirit in order to revive the spirit of the lowly and to revive the heart of the contrite."
ISAIAH 57:15 NASB

Father, You're holy. You're set apart from everyone and everything, yet You still chose to dwell with humans. You sent Your Son into this world as a human, and Your Holy Spirit lives in all who put their trust in You. I love the way You've chosen me to be Yours. When I'm feeling down, You revive my spirit. When I'm feeling regret and remorse, You're ready to revive my heart. So much in this world seems to suck the life right out of me. I get worn out and feel tempted to worry. But You are ready to revive. You give life—as the Creator You give physical life, and through Jesus You give spiritual life. I'm grateful You are such a giving God. Thank You for reviving me and filling my life and spirit with Your great love. In Jesus' name I pray. Amen.

Trust vs. Trouble

*"Do not let your heart be troubled. You have put
your trust in God, put your trust in Me also."*
JOHN 14:1 NLV

Lord Jesus, I'm so thankful You're trustworthy. Because
You have proven Yourself to be faithful and true, I can put
my trust in You. When I do, I don't have to be worried or
afraid! My heart doesn't have to be troubled. I can find
rest from all my concerns and feel at peace. I don't have
to feel like I'm the one needing to do all of the work or
make sure things need to work out the right way. I can trust
that You're working out all the details in a wonderful way.
Even when life's uncertain, You have it all under control.
I don't have to worry! That is a huge, comforting gift that
makes me happy. Thank You! I want to keep trusting You
even when I'm tempted to try to make things go my way.
Help me step back and remember that You're God and
I'm not. You have a good plan and purpose that You're
working out. I can't wait to see what You do in my life! In
Your holy name I pray. Amen.

The Ugliness of Fighting

*A dry piece of food with peace and quiet is
better than a house full of food with fighting.*
PROVERBS 17:1 NLV

Father God, conflict should never be a surprise. I'll never
get along with everyone, and not everyone will get along
with me. You've created everyone to have their own unique
perspectives and opinions. Just because I should expect
conflict though, it doesn't make living through it any easier or enjoyable. In fact, fighting feels pretty awful. The
proverb is right: it's better to eat just a dry piece of food
in a peaceful, quiet place, instead of feasting on all sorts
of delicious food in a home where people are fighting.
Could You please help me remember this the next time
I want to start or continue an argument with my family
members? I don't want to start a fight, and I don't want
to become the sort of person who needs to get the last
word. Help me make peace in my home a priority. In Jesus'
name I pray. Amen.

Choosing Good

Turn away from what is sinful. Do what is good. Look for peace and go after it.
1 PETER 3:11 NLV

Lord, whether I realize it or not, every day I make choices between what is good and what is sinful. All the time I need to choose things like what to eat, what to say, what to watch, what to talk about, what to listen to, how well I do my chores or my schoolwork, and how I treat other people. Please help me to honor You in each decision. I could choose sin, or I could turn away from what I know is wrong. I want to do good! Sometimes I'm tempted to do what's comfortable or easy. Sometimes I just want to feel good instead of doing good. Other times I want to fit in instead of standing up for what's right or trying to go after peace. Even when it's difficult, and even if a lot of people are upset or disappointed with my decision, please help me stick to my convictions and do what is good. I want to do what's right in Your eyes. In Jesus' name I pray. Amen.

Saved, Not Shaken

My soul is quiet and waits for God alone. He is the One Who saves me. He alone is my rock and the One Who saves me. He is my strong place. I will not be shaken.
PSALM 62:1-2 NLV

Oh Lord, so often I rush around and try to do things on my own. I'm impatient. I want to rush through life. I want to be busy and do, do, do all the time. It's hard to quiet myself down and wait. But You are the One who saves me. You are the One I can and should wait for and trust. You're my rock. You're my strong place. Because of You I don't need to worry or fear. I can stand strong in You. I won't be moved or shaken. That kind of stability is pretty amazing and so very comforting. If I depended only on myself, I'd be moved and shaken and upset. But I can depend on You. I can put all my confidence in You, because You'll never ever let me down. Thank You!

Shout for Joy!

Shout for joy, you heavens; rejoice, you earth; burst into song, you mountains! For the LORD comforts his people and will have compassion on his afflicted ones.
ISAIAH 49:13 NIV

Lord God, You are so very good! Your goodness goes way beyond me or even all people. Your goodness affects everything on earth and stretches up to the heavens. All creation can rejoice in You! You comfort Your people. When Your loved ones suffer, You shower them with Your love. You look on me with mercy and kindness. Far too often, I take Your blessings for granted. I don't stop to marvel at Your great love and patience and faithfulness. I forget how good Your goodness is or how kind Your kindness is. I need to praise You! I shout for joy over the wonderful ways You work in my life. I want to rejoice in You! I worship You, mighty God! I praise Your name, my Lord and Savior!

Not My Own Power

My message and my preaching were not with wise and persuasive words, but with a demonstration of the Spirit's power, so that your faith might not rest on human wisdom, but on God's power.

1 CORINTHIANS 2:4–5 NIV

Father, You are so very powerful! I'm grateful that You're willing to use some of Your power in my life. I know I'm not the best at everything. Even if I try my hardest, I fail. And sometimes I feel pretty weak and powerless. I want You to use me in this world though. Even with all my failures and flaws, could You please strengthen me? Could You please give me the words and energy to do Your work? I want to rely on Your Holy Spirit to fill me, strengthen me, and provide all I need. As He does, I'm excited to watch my faith in You grow. I know I can only do so much—or, actually, so little—on my own. I can hardly wait to see all that You can do through me! Please use me in any way. I want to honor You with all of my life. In Jesus' name I ask these things. Amen.

Comfort after Troubles

Though you have made me see troubles, many and bitter, you will restore my life again; from the depths of the earth you will again bring me up. You will increase my honor and comfort me once more.

PSALM 71:20–21 NIV

Father, You've never promised a problem-free life. In fact, Jesus told His followers that in this world they would have troubles. Sometimes problems seem to pile up while other times seem to be smooth sailing. When I'm going through a really rough time and it feels like the challenges and bad news just won't stop, I believe those struggles won't last forever. You'll restore my life. You'll increase my honor. And what might be sweetest of all is the way You'll comfort me. I won't have to feel I'm all on my own dealing with my problems, but You'll comfort me with Your love. After going through hard times, the good times will seem even better. For that I'm thankful! Thanks for never leaving me and for carrying me through all of my life—good times *and* bad times. In Jesus' name I pray. Amen.

Making Every Effort

*Make every effort to live in peace with everyone and
to be holy; without holiness no one will see the Lord.*
HEBREWS 12:14 NIV

Lord, You've called Your followers to holy living to show
our love and devotion to You. You're perfect in goodness,
and it makes sense that Your followers should try to be
like You. You know I'm imperfect, Lord, and as much as
I'd like to live like You, I'm weak and get frustrated by my
failures. I don't always make the right choices, but I still
should keep trying. I don't have to give up just because
I mess up. Instead, please help me try again. As difficult
as it may feel, please help me live in peace with other
people, especially people who think and behave so much
differently than I do. Instead of focusing on our differences,
please help me to love them like You do. Please help me
truly make every effort to live in a way that shows my love
and honor for You. In Jesus' name I ask all of this. Amen.

Strong and Courageous

Be strong and let your heart take courage,
all you who wait for the LORD.
PSALM 31:24 NASB

Father God, sometimes I feel really nervous and uncertain and afraid. I don't know what will happen. And sometimes I really just dread what I know I need to do. In those times when I feel like my courage has vanished, please strengthen me in an amazing way. When I feel scared, please give me courage to do what's right and whatever I need to do. I want to trust You, and I know I can. While I wait for You in trust, I want my heart and soul and mind to take courage in You alone. You are my strength and my song. I don't need to trust in myself or my own understanding of things. Instead, I choose to trust in You. You are my tower of strength. You are the rock that won't be moved. I worship You alone! In Jesus' strong name I pray. Amen.

Quiet Trust

*The Lord God, the Holy One of Israel, has said,
"In turning away from sin and in rest, you will
be saved. Your strength will come by being
quiet and by trusting." But you would not.*
ISAIAH 30:15 NLV

Lord God, You've specifically pointed out that when I rest in You and turn away from sin, I'll be saved. Strength will come by being quiet and trusting. I have a choice either to listen to Your good Word or to go my own way. If I don't trust You, if I keep my sinful habits, and if I work, work, work to try to save myself, I won't be saved at all. I want to trust You! I want to be still and know that You are God. Like Jesus taught, He gives rest. When I learn from Him, I'll find rest for my soul. I want to learn from Him! I want to trust You completely. I want to turn away from what I think is my own wisdom or the world's wisdom and turn to You. Help me quiet my soul and wait for You. In Jesus' gentle and humble name I pray. Amen.

Why Worry?

*"Can any one of you by worrying
add a single hour to your life?"*
MATTHEW 6:27 NIV

Lord Jesus, You taught that worry doesn't change a thing. If anything, it takes away peace of mind and piles on stress. Situations can't be changed if I worry about them. When I feel tempted to worry, could You please remind me of this? I want to be worry-free! In fact, deep down I think it would be great to have such a strong and certain faith in You that I wouldn't fear anything that comes my way. Please help me trust You more and more. I want to keep my eyes on You and not on the circumstances and situations around me. Please help me to be aware that You are working wonders all the time, even when I can't see what You are doing. Thank You for loving me like You do and freeing me from worry. In Your precious name I pray. Amen.

Quiet Down!

The words of the wise heard in calm are better than the shouting of a ruler among fools.

ECCLESIASTES 9:17 NASB

Father, sometimes I lose my temper. I don't think before I speak or react. Sometimes I get so upset, I scream and shout and throw a fit. Could You please help me grow out of these temper tantrums? Could You please help me get my emotions under control? I don't want to get upset, and I don't want to hurt others' feelings by what I say or do in the heat of the moment. Please help me grow in self-control. And please calm me down. I'd love to grow up in wisdom and outgrow my foolishness. Please help my words and emotions and reactions reflect my love and respect for You and the way You're working in my heart. In Jesus' name I pray. Amen.

Let Your Light Shine

"You are the light of the world. A city set on a hill cannot be hidden; nor do people light a lamp and put it under a basket, but on the lampstand, and it gives light to all who are in the house. Your light must shine before people in such a way that they may see your good works, and glorify your Father who is in heaven."

MATTHEW 5:14–16 NASB

Father, I know You are the one true God. I know that through Jesus You've provided rescue from the consequences of sin. I know Your Holy Spirit lives in me. All of that wonderful truth lights me up. I don't want to keep Your light hidden from others. No matter what happens in this world, please help me to be bold enough to display Your light for all to see. I want other people to glorify You because of the good things I do. I want to shine like a light in this world! Help me do really good things day after day to help Your light shine even brighter. I love You, Lord! In Jesus' name I pray. Amen.

My Reliance

You are my strength, I sing praise to you; you,
God, are my fortress, my God on whom I can rely.
PSALM 59:17 NIV

God, You are my God! I can and do rely on You. You are my safe place. You're my fortress of strength! No matter what happens in the world around me, I can cling to You. I praise You because my strength is found in You. I praise You because You are faithful. You are constant. Everything in this world may be uncertain, but You are certain. Everything in this world may change, but You are unchanging. Without You, I'd feel like my whole life was shaky, but I can stand firm in my faith. Because of You, I don't have to fear. Lord, I know I can rely completely on You. When I'm tempted to rely on myself, please help me step back and remember who You are. I can rely on You, my safe, strong defender. In Jesus' strong name I pray. Amen.

It's Gardening Time!

Sow for yourselves, with a view to righteousness; harvest in accordance with kindness. Break up your uncultivated ground, for it is time to seek the LORD until He comes and rains righteousness on you.

HOSEA 10:12 NASB

Father, thank You for filling the Bible with so many practical examples. Good, righteous living doesn't need to be a mystery. In fact, You explain it so I can understand. I want to plant good habits and decisions in my life that will result in righteousness. In a kind and gentle way, I want to gather the good things that are formed because of my right choices and good works. If there's any part of my life that's unchecked or hardened by sin, please help me break it up. I want the soil of my heart to be good so that when You rain Your righteousness on me, all that I've faithfully planted will bloom and grow. I want my obedience and love for You to affect every single part of my life.

Come

As Jesus walked beside the Sea of Galilee, he saw
Simon and his brother Andrew casting a net into the
lake, for they were fishermen. "Come, follow me,"
Jesus said, "and I will send you out to fish for people."
At once they left their nets and followed him.
MARK 1:16–18 NIV

Lord Jesus, when You walked on this earth, people knew You were different from others. There was something remarkable about You. You were God! In the flesh! All You needed to do was say the word—"Come!"—and people left everything they knew to follow You. Today You ask me to come and follow You too. I want to leave everything behind—including my hopes and expectations—to follow You. As I follow You, please teach me how to be a fisher of people. How can I bring others into a relationship with You? How can I help gather souls like fish in a net? Please guide me and give me plenty of grace as I try to walk by faith in You. In Your holy name I pray. Amen.

Strength of Heart

Say to those whose heart is afraid, "Have strength of heart, and do not be afraid. See, your God will come ready to punish. He will come to make sinners pay for their sins, but He will save you."
ISAIAH 35:4 NLV

Father God, I bow before You in worship. You are the One true God who has created all things and knows all things. You hold all things together. You know who accepts and trusts You and who doesn't. You've promised to save those who believe in You. Even when I feel afraid and get scared of what's happening around me, I can have a strong heart. Fear seems to be such a normal part of this life. So much is said and done with people being afraid of what might happen. But I don't have to fear! I can and do trust that You'll save me, just as You've promised. You'll also make the evil pay for all that they do in this life. So even when heartless people scheme evil plans, I don't have to worry. You'll take care of me. Please help me to do what's right in Your sight. I want to find my strength in You and You alone. Please develop a strength of heart in me. In Jesus' strong name I pray. Amen.

What Is Right

Turn away from the sinful things young people want to do. Go after what is right. Have a desire for faith and love and peace. Do this with those who pray to God from a clean heart.
2 TIMOTHY 2:22 NLV

Lord God, there's so much in this world I could do. And there's so much temptation to do things that wouldn't please You. It's no surprise to You that there are so many ways I could choose to sin. But even if it doesn't always seem fun or popular, I want to go after what's right. Even when young people go after the sinful things they want to do, please help me turn away from them. I want to have a clean heart in Your sight. You can help me grow in love and peace. Would You please do it, Lord? Could You please help my faith grow? I want to be more like You, but it's hard in this world. So please help me. I love You and want to honor You with my whole life. In Jesus' name I pray. Amen.

No Stumbling

*Those who love Your Law have great peace,
and nothing causes them to stumble.*
PSALM 119:165 NASB

Father, Your Word is absolutely true. You've given it to us to help us know how to live right. It's not like You created us then left us on our own to try to figure everything out. No, You've told us specifically what to do and what not to do. If and when we follow You and obey, our lives are filled with blessings and life. Lord, I want life! And I would love for You to surprise me over and over with Your blessings. I also would love to experience great peace. I don't want to worry. I don't want to get all stressed out. I want to live every day with a quiet reassurance and peace of mind that You're in control. Because of You and Your goodness, I don't have to fear. Because of You and the way Your Word lays out the right ways of living, I don't need to fumble and stumble around. Thank You! I'm grateful for Your clear direction. In Jesus' name I pray. Amen.

Peaceful Rest

My people will live in peaceful dwelling places,
in secure homes, in undisturbed places of rest.
ISAIAH 32:18 NIV

Lord God, thank You for promising Your people peace. I don't have to worry about what might happen to me. You'll give me rest! No matter how this world rages, no matter what people say or do to me, You'll still give me peace. You offer protection like nothing or no one else. I don't have to fear. I also don't have to stick to myself, soak up all Your peace and rest, and do nothing. No, I can boldly go out into the world for You. I can be the hands and feet of Jesus every day to the people around me. I can treat others with Your kindness and gentleness. I can love the unlovable because of You. I can be so full of Your joy and peace that it spills out of my life to those around me. I want to be Your representative in this lost and lonely world. I want to be Your voice of hope and peace in the middle of all the confusion and chaos. Please give me opportunities to trust You in faith then feel refreshed by Your sweet gift of rest. In Your holy name I ask all of this. Amen.

Happy!

I am not saying I need anything. I have learned to be happy with whatever I have.
PHILIPPIANS 4:11 NLV

Father, You're the giver of all good gifts. Thank You for all You've given me! You truly have blessed me with so much—from basic needs like food and a place to live to special relationships, to the amazing talents and strengths I have. Sometimes I take Your good gifts for granted. I might even think I want different things. But when I keep in mind that You have a specific purpose for my life, I know You've created me in a unique way. All that I have has been given to me for a reason. I want to be happy with whatever You've given me. Since I don't truly need anything, I pray I can be thankful with what I have. Please help me learn to identify when I want something versus when I actually need something. And please help me see how very much I have. Please soften and shape my heart so I'm willing to share Your blessings and gifts with others. In Jesus' name I pray. Amen.

Given New Life

*"The Lord your God is with you, a Powerful One
Who wins the battle. He will have much joy over
you. With His love He will give you new life.
He will have joy over you with loud singing."*
ZEPHANIAH 3:17 NLV

Lord God, sometimes I feel so weak and helpless, like my life doesn't matter in the big scheme of things. What can You really accomplish through my life? Do I help or hurt Your work in this world? Yet Your Word tells the truth about how You find joy in me. Joy! So much joy, in fact, that You have joy over me with loud singing. And with Your love for me, You give me new life. Your joy and love are wonderful things. Please help me experience them today. As I do, I need to remember who You are—so powerful and so far above and beyond anything in this world. But You're with me. And You're so powerful You win the battle. That's a huge relief! I'm thankful I can trust in You and find rest for my soul. I love You, Lord!

Throw It Off

Since we are surrounded by such a great cloud of witnesses, let us throw off everything that hinders and the sin that so easily entangles. And let us run with perseverance the race marked out for us, fixing our eyes on Jesus, the pioneer and perfecter of faith.
HEBREWS 12:1–2 NIV

Lord Jesus, I want to fix my eyes on You! It's so difficult in this world though. I'm pulled in different directions. I face a lot of temptations. But some of those things are just obstacles. I get tangled up in other sins until I trip and fall. I want to break free from those distractions, and I want to focus on You. Please help me run the race of my life well. If my life is a marathon, please help me run with endurance. Help me persevere when I get tired. Help me stay in my lane and not get distracted by what's happening in other people's lives or the world around me. That kind of focus is tough, but I know You can help me. Thank You for beginning my faith, Jesus, and thank You for working in and through me to perfect my faith. I love You!

Even When You Sleep

You rise up early, and go to bed late, and work hard for your food, all for nothing. For the Lord gives to His loved ones even while they sleep.
PSALM 127:2 NLV

Lord, it's amazingly comforting to know that I don't have to work for my blessings. You give to me so generously, and I don't need to do a thing to earn or deserve Your goodness. When I'm tempted to get up early and stay up late just to cram in all of my work, please remind me that all of that effort is meaningless. You love me, and You give to those You love even while they sleep. That might be one of the sweetest things I've realized in a long time: You choose to give me good gifts even while I sleep! I don't have to do a thing. Thank You. I pray I'll spend my time awake enjoying and seeking You more instead of working and striving for Your approval and love. You love me anyway! Thank You! With a heart full of thankfulness, I praise You.

Wise or Foolish

Understanding is a fountain of life to those who have it, but the discipline of fools is foolishness.
PROVERBS 16:22 NASB

Father, it's hard to realize that every choice I make means I'm either one step closer to being wise or a fool. Some days I just want to have fun. I want to forget about any consequences, and I'd rather totally enjoy myself and make spontaneous choices. Life seems so much more fun that way! Remembering that every choice I make actually does have consequences kills my enthusiasm. But the thing is, the more foolish choices I make, the more of a fool I'll become. I'll also need to face up to a bunch of avoidable consequences. Even if it makes me less than popular with my friends, please help me use my brain before doing things. Help me grow in wisdom so I can make wise, responsible choices. As I do that, please help me have fun too. Following the rules or making the best choices doesn't need to mean that life is totally boring. Please help me trust You for what's right and enjoy the rewards that come with wise choices! In Jesus' name I pray. Amen.

Do You Have the Life?

*The testimony is this, that God has given us
eternal life, and this life is in His Son. The one who
has the Son has the life; the one who does not
have the Son of God does not have the life.*

1 JOHN 5:11-12 NASB

Father, thank You for explaining what I need to do to have eternal life. Something so big—forever life with You!—seems like it should be complicated. But eternal life is found in Your Son, Jesus. If I have the Son of God, I have eternal life. If I don't have the Son of God, I don't have eternal life. It's that simple. To be sure I do have Him, right now I'll say that I absolutely believe that Jesus is Lord. I believe You raised Him from the dead and He's alive today. I believe that only through Christ I can spend eternity with You. Salvation doesn't come by the good things I do, so it doesn't matter if I try really hard. It doesn't come by any other name or religion. It's only through Your Son. Thank You for His forever life! In Jesus' name I pray. Amen.

Searching for Wisdom

Blessed are those who find wisdom, those who gain understanding, for she is more profitable than silver and yields better returns than gold. She is more precious than rubies; nothing you desire can compare with her.
PROVERBS 3:13–15 NIV

Father, over and over Your Word tells about how priceless wisdom is. It's better to be wise than a fool, and making wise choices will bring wonderful results in my life. I have to admit that choosing wisely can feel like a sacrifice though. When I see people around me living for the moment and doing what feels good, it's tempting to follow the crowd. And so many voices compete for my attention. Please help me shut out all the noise and focus on You. If something is foolish, please help me spy the folly right away. Please help me recognize the treasure found in wisdom. It's worth more than silver and even gold. It's more precious than jewels. None of the stuff of this world can compare with wisdom's riches. While it's sometimes hard for me to see that right now as I try to figure out good choices for my life, please help me begin to see how I'll change for the better because of wisdom. In Jesus' name I pray. Amen.

The Gift of Peace

May the Lord of peace himself give you peace at all times and in every way. The Lord be with all of you.
2 THESSALONIANS 3:16 NIV

Lord, peace seems like such a nice thought. With peace, I don't have to worry if anyone's upset with me, I'm not in the middle of disagreements, and I don't feel troubled. I don't even need to feel stressed out about my future. Everything just seems nice and calm. I feel refreshed from the inside out. This kind of peace doesn't only have to be a dream though. You are the Lord of peace, and You can give peace. The peace You offer isn't a short-lived, onetime offer. You give peace at all times and in every way. And peace isn't the only thing You so generously give. You give Yourself too! The apostle Paul knew he could ask the Lord to be with people. You can be with me! And when You're with me, I'll experience Your peace no matter what I'm going through in my day. Thanks for Your peace! I don't understand it, but I love the way it makes me feel. In Jesus' name I pray. Amen.

Behaving Myself

Consider the blameless, observe the upright;
a future awaits those who seek peace.
PSALM 37:37 NIV

Father, for most of my childhood, and even today, I don't like other people telling me to behave myself. Sometimes—okay, *most* times!—I like doing what I feel like doing. But Your Word tells me that good things will happen to those who behave. If I make right choices, I'm on a good path in life. When I seek peace with other people and in this world, I can look forward to my future. Could You please help me with this kind of blameless, right, peaceful living? Because it's hard! I don't always feel like living that way, and it's hard to make right choices all the time. It's hard not to argue and fight with people, especially when they're treating me badly. And it's hard to behave myself so I can live a life without blame. But with You and Your help, I can do anything. Please help me! In Jesus' name I pray. Amen.

He's the One

*LORD, you establish peace for us; all that we
have accomplished you have done for us.*
ISAIAH 26:12 NIV

Lord, You're the One who establishes peace. And You're the One who has plans and purposes for my life and then makes them happen. When I really believe this, it frees me up so much! I don't have to be consumed with trying to do more and be more. I don't need to obsess over how I'm doing my best at school or what I can do to help my friendships and other relationships. Ultimately I need to trust You. When I start feeling worried and stressed, I need to stop and pray. You're the Difference Maker. I can take a deep breath and trust You. When I do trust You, I can truly rest in my trust. Thank You for working in my life! I pray I'll try to spy the little and big ways You're working. I know You'll lead me along paths of peace to accomplish what You have planned. Please help me follow You! In Jesus' name I pray. Amen.

Don't Be So Judgmental!

There is only one Lawgiver and Judge,
the one who is able to save and destroy.
But you—who are you to judge your neighbor?
JAMES 4:12 NIV

Father God, I confess I don't always remember that You are the one Lawgiver, and You are the one Judge. It's so easy for me to judge other people. All it takes is looking at other people, and instantly I can start comparing them. I notice so much so quickly, from clothing choices to hairstyles. I notice attitudes and the way other people talk or walk. It's like I can't turn my brain off, and my observations end up shaping my opinions. And so often those opinions turn into judgment. The thing is, I don't know what's going on in a person's life or heart or mind until I stop to get to know her and actually ask questions. But do I usually do that? Not as often as I should. Please help me stop judging other people. Please help me to be more understanding. I want to be an encourager and a helper instead of a judge. In Jesus' name I pray. Amen.

The Giver of Rest

But now the Lord my God has given me rest on every side. There is no trouble or anything bad happening.
1 KINGS 5:4 NLV

Lord, my God, You're the giver of good gifts! And You're the giver of rest and peace. Just like You gave King Solomon rest and peace during his reign, could You please give me rest? Could You please fill my life and relationships with peace? I'd love a break from trouble, and I would love for nothing bad to happen. I know that every life includes some kind of trouble and challenge, because that's what shapes a person. And I know that You can bring goodness and growth out of any conflict and crisis. I completely trust You for that! But even when I experience struggles, please also bless my life with Your goodness. Please fill my life with Your rest. In Jesus' name I pray. Amen.

When I Don't Want to Love

"You have heard that it was said, 'Love your neighbor and hate your enemy.' But I tell you, love your enemies and pray for those who persecute you."
MATTHEW 5:43–44 NIV

Father, I don't like having enemies. In fact, when I know someone doesn't like me or says awful things about me, I get pretty mad and defensive. Who do they think they are? Why don't they see things my way? My natural reaction is to react in anger and hurt. But that's not what Jesus taught. Jesus taught something very uncomfortable: I'm supposed to love people who oppose me. He specifically said to love my enemies and pray for my persecutors. I have to admit that it's really hard to hear and even harder to do. But I want to obey You and be Your ambassador in this world. Please help me love others, whether they are my neighbors or my enemies. Please fill me with Your love so I can show it to people around me. In Jesus' name I pray. Amen.

Comfort in Suffering

*My comfort in my suffering is this: Your
promise preserves my life.*
PSALM 119:50 NIV

O Lord, some days are just bad. I know I probably should try to find good in everything, but sometimes I feel pretty down. A lot of things can make me feel depressed, and it's hard to find a bright spot. You can be my bright spot though. You can be my good thing. When I'm suffering, I can find comfort in Your promises. In Your Word, You promise You'll never leave me or forsake me. You have called me by name. I am Yours! When I pass through rushing waters, You will be with me. They won't drown me. When I walk through fire, I will not be scorched, for You are the Lord my God, the Holy One, my Savior. Those promises preserve my life like nothing else. Please help me find comfort in them even right now. In Jesus' holy name I pray. Amen.

What's Your Treasure?

"Do not store up for yourselves treasures on earth, where moth and rust destroy, and where thieves break in and steal. But store up for yourselves treasures in heaven, where neither moth nor rust destroys, and where thieves do not break in or steal; for where your treasure is, there your heart will be also."

MATTHEW 6:19–21 NASB

Father, it's really easy to focus on things of this world. I see so much every day, and I'm asked to buy so many things. It's like all I see around me is what other people own or bigger and better stuff. I'm so used to seeing advertisements and being encouraged not to be content with what I already have. So much of this world focuses on storing up treasures and belongings here on earth. But You've asked me to store up treasure that won't fall apart. Instead, if I store up treasures in heaven, they'll last forever. Father, please help me treasure heavenly things instead of earthly things. I want my heart to be with You, set on treasures that will last forever. In Jesus' name I pray. Amen.

Safety in the Storm

God is our safe place and our strength. He is always our help when we are in trouble. So we will not be afraid, even if the earth is shaken and the mountains fall into the center of the sea, and even if its waters go wild with storm and the mountains shake with its action.

PSALM 46:1–3 NLV

Lord, I admit I get scared when I hear about natural disasters. Earthquakes and hurricanes are scary things; and when I hear about disasters that happen around the world, I wonder what I would do if I was in the middle of an epic storm. The amazing thing about You though, is that You are my safe place. And You are my strength. When I'm in trouble, You're always my help. So when scary things happen like natural disasters, horrible weather, and personal crises in my life, I don't have to worry about any of it. You'll keep me safe. You'll make a way for me, even when the world around me rages. Thank You for being my safe place! I choose to trust in You. It's such a huge relief that because of You, I don't have to be afraid. In Jesus' safe, strong name I pray. Amen.

Safe

He will come and feed His flock in the strength of the Lord, in the great power of the name of the Lord His God. His people will live there and be safe, because at that time He will be great to the ends of the earth.

MICAH 5:4 NLV

Lord, I love the way Your Word describes Jesus, all the way from the Old Testament through the New Testament. And I love the way He brings hope and comfort to His flock. Thank You that I can be safe through Jesus. Thank You that He feeds His flock of followers in Your strength and the great power of Your name. Absolutely nothing on this earth compares with that. When I find myself getting caught up in the cares and worries of this world, please help me remember Your greatness. Help me keep my problems in perspective. They might seem like big deals right now, but in light of Your power and strength, I don't need to be concerned. Please change my heart and mind to keep You—not myself—high and lifted up. In Jesus' strong name I pray. Amen.

Set Apart

May the God of peace set you apart for Himself.
May every part of you be set apart for God.
May your spirit and your soul and your body
be kept complete. May you be without blame
when our Lord Jesus Christ comes again.
1 THESSALONIANS 5:23 NLV

Father God, so often I feel like the world is trying to press me into some pattern. I'm asked to think or speak a certain way and do specific things. If I'm not like the world, people make fun of me, either behind my back or to my face. When I try to be myself and stand up for my beliefs, someone tries to change me. But I don't want to be more like the world, Lord. I want to be more like You. I want You to set me apart for Yourself. Please help me keep every part of myself set apart for You. In Your goodness and Your divine protection, please keep my spirit, soul, and body complete. I would love to be blameless when Jesus returns. It's hard though, and it feels like it keeps getting harder. No matter the cost, I want to stay set apart for You. Please give me strength and guidance to do that. In Jesus' name I pray. Amen.

Wait!

*Wait for the LORD; be strong and let your
heart take courage; yes, wait for the LORD.*
PSALM 27:14 NASB

Lord, waiting is so hard! I don't feel very patient, and I really don't like waiting for anything. I'd like almost instant results and answers. But You tell me to wait. Even the Psalms answer my question: *Do I really have to wait?* Yes! Wait for the Lord. And so I'll wait for You because You tell me to, and I don't have much of a choice. Please give me strength in my waiting and strength as I learn to be patient. Please help my heart to be courageous too. Strong and courageous is what I need to be, even when it feels so difficult. I believe You're with me though. I can hardly wait to see what You'll work and accomplish in my life. I trust You, and I love You. In Jesus' name I pray. Amen.

What Will Right Living Do?

The fruit of that righteousness will be peace;
its effect will be quietness and confidence forever.

ISAIAH 32:17 NIV

Father, over and over in Your Word, You tell me that right living, or righteousness, is what I should choose. It's hard to choose not to go my own way and choose Your way instead. When I do choose righteousness, good things will come! It's like I'm a fruit tree that will produce good fruit. Right living produces peace, and that's so much better than worry, fear, or struggle. Peace is what I'd love. Right living doesn't just help me experience peace, but I'll also have confidence, security, and trust. That sounds amazing! A righteous life will bring the gift of quietness too. A life without noisy distractions would bring a lot of peace. I could actually hear myself think, and I'll be able to listen to You much more easily. All of these benefits of righteousness sound pretty good to me! Could You please help me discern between right and wrong choices? Thank You! In Jesus' name I pray. Amen.

Happy with What I Have

Keep your lives free from the love of money.
Be happy with what you have. God has said,
"I will never leave you or let you be alone."

HEBREWS 13:5 NLV

Lord, so much of this world screams at me to want more. I should want different and better things. I don't have enough. I deserve to get what I want when I want it. I can have it all. But those lies are so different from the truth You offer. I don't need more. I don't need different things or "upgraded" anything. I will keep surviving if I don't get what catches my eye. If I have to wait to get something, it won't be the end of the world. And even if I had it all—whatever that "all" is—I still might not be completely satisfied. Instead of buying into what the world tells me, please help me listen to You. Help me to be happy with what I have. And instead of being jealous and wanting so much more, please help me not to love money or the things money can buy. If I do have a lot of possessions, please help me to be generous and willingly share with others. In Jesus' name I pray. Amen.

Who Are You Pleasing?

When the ways of a man are pleasing
to the Lord, He makes even those who
hate him to be at peace with him.
PROVERBS 16:7 NLV

Lord, I don't want to be a people pleaser. It's hard though, because people demand so much from me—especially my time and attention. And a big part of me feels like I need to perform or make others happy. If I end up as a disappointment, will they love me as much? Will I find approval in their eyes? The huge truth bomb is that I need to be concerned about pleasing You and not people. When I please You, You do a great thing: You make people be at peace with me! It doesn't matter if they're people who love or hate me. You pave the way for me to experience peace. Because of that—and the fact that You're God!—I want to please You with what I say and do and even think. Please help me understand how I can choose ways that please You. In Jesus' name I pray. Amen.

A Great Multitude

After these things I looked, and behold, a great multitude which no one could count, from every nation and all the tribes, peoples, and languages, standing before the throne and before the Lamb, clothed in white robes, and palm branches were in their hands; and they cried out with a loud voice, saying, "Salvation belongs to our God who sits on the throne, and to the Lamb."
REVELATION 7:9–10 NASB

Lord God, salvation belongs to You! And salvation belongs to Your Son, the Lamb of God who takes away the sin of the world. When I think about what heaven will be like, I'm excited to praise You forever with people from every nation, tribe, and tongue. No one will look the same. No one will sound the same. You've called so many people to be Your own from all over the world. Even though we'll look and sound different, we'll all have one thing in common: we will praise You! Thank You for calling us. Thank You for calling me to be Your daughter! I love You, and I'm so glad I get to spend eternity seeing Your majesty, being near You, and praising You. In Jesus' holy, awesome name I pray. Amen.

My Rescuer

He took me away from the powerful one
who fights against me, and from those who
hated me. They were too strong for me.

PSALM 18:17 NLV

Father, in the Bible there are plenty of accounts of King David's life. It wasn't easy! He had many enemies who hated him so much they wanted to kill him. Yet You protected him. You kept him safe. No matter what they plotted against David, You ruined their plans so that he died an old man. When hard times come in my life—and they will!—please remind me that You're my protector. You'll rescue me. You'll ruin the schemes of my enemies. You'll even keep me safe from people who hate me and want to fight against me. When I'm tempted to worry and take matters into my own hands, I want to step back and let You be God. I want to watch You work in amazing ways. Please continue to protect me. My trust is in You! In Jesus' name I pray. Amen.

The Lord Will Be between Us

Jonathan said to David, "Go in peace. For we have promised each other in the name of the Lord, saying, 'The Lord will be between me and you, and between my children and your children forever.'"
1 SAMUEL 20:42 NLV

Father, I'm so thankful for the gift of friendship. Thank You for blessing me with friends. Even if I have just a few close friends, I'm thankful for the way they help me get through life. Could You please help me to be a good friend? And could You please bring friends into my life who totally love You? It would be amazing to have a friend who points me to You. I pray for forever friends too. Even if I have no idea who might end up being a part of my life for years and years, I pray that even now You'd start strengthening our friendship. In Jesus' name I pray. Amen.

Falling Down in Worship

All the angels were standing around the throne and around the elders and the four living creatures. They fell down on their faces before the throne and worshiped God, saying: "Amen! Praise and glory and wisdom and thanks and honor and power and strength be to our God for ever and ever. Amen!"
REVELATION 7:11–12 NIV

Lord, You alone are awesome and amazing! Nothing in this world can compare to You. Because of Your greatness, You deserve praise forever and ever. So when Revelation tells how the angels will fall down on their faces and worship You, I want to join with them. In all I say and do, I want to bring glory to Your name! I praise You! You are all-wise and all-powerful. You are infinitely strong. Thank You for all You've done throughout history, all You've done to save Your people, and all You've done in my life. You are worthy of honor and praise forever and ever. Amen!

He Has Great Plans for You

O Lord, You are my God. I will praise You. I will give thanks to Your name. For You have been faithful to do great things, plans that You made long ago.

ISAIAH 25:1 NLV

O Lord, You are my God! I praise You! Thank You for choosing me to be Yours. Thank You for doing amazing things in my life. Even if I don't always remember or realize it, You have a plan and a purpose for me. Long before I was born, You planned great things for my life. That's mind blowing! Because You have plans for me, I can trust You. I'm so thankful I don't have to muddle through this world in my own strength or in my own wisdom. I'm so grateful I can turn to You and rely on You. Your faithful love and the way You provide for me brings me so much comfort. I love You!

Good News of Peace

*Then Christ came and preached the Good News
of peace to you who were far away from God.
And He preached it to us who were near God.*
EPHESIANS 2:17 NLV

Lord Jesus, thank You for coming to earth to rescue people from the judgment of sin. Thank You for bringing Your Good News of peace. In fact, You are the Good News of peace. You didn't exclude anyone from Your Good News—You brought it to people who were far from God and close to God. It didn't matter if they were young or old, man or woman, rich or poor, sick or well. You've gladly offered Your rescue to absolutely anyone. Because of You, Your death, and Your life after death, I can be made alive in You. When I say that You are Lord and fully believe God the Father raised You from the dead, I'm saved and made alive in You. That's Good News! Thank You so much for what You've done and for how You've made this truth available to absolutely anyone and everyone. In Your name I pray. Amen.

Following the Rules

The law of the LORD is perfect, refreshing the soul. The statutes of the LORD are trustworthy, making wise the simple.

Lord, as much as I may not always be happy about needing to follow someone else's rules, instructions are a very good thing! As long as they're right and true, good instruction can lead me to a better life. Please help me remember that Your law is a very good thing. In fact, it's perfect! Following Your rules will refresh my soul and make me wiser. I can trust what You've told me to do and what not to do. I need to make sure I read the Bible more and more so that I know what Your law is. While I could wait for someone else to teach me, I'm so glad that I can also learn it on my own. Thank You for Your Word! Thank You for wanting to guide me to a better life instead of leaving me to try to figure things out on my own. In Jesus' holy name I pray. Amen.

Beautiful!

How beautiful on the mountains are the feet of
him who brings good news, who tells of peace
and brings good news of happiness, who tells of
saving power, and says to Zion, "Your God rules!"
ISAIAH 52:7 NLV

Lord God, I want to become a beautiful woman, but not like the world classifies beauty. Right now it seems like there's so much emphasis on looks and what outward beauty is. But what a person looks like on the outside doesn't last. Fads change and people get old. What won't change is my inner beauty. If I can become beautiful on the inside, that will last until my dying day. When I tell other people about Your Good News, I tell about the peace that comes from You. Your Good News brings happiness and saving power that others don't have. When I tell other people about Your peace, I become more and more beautiful from my head all the way to my toes. When I tell other people about You so they can come to know You, my beauty grows. Please help me become beautiful in this way! Amen.

Want Some More?

Then he said to them, "Watch out! Be on your
guard against all kinds of greed; life does not
consist in an abundance of possessions."

LUKE 12:15 NIV

Lord Jesus, during Your time on earth, You knew what motivated and captivated humans. You knew greed was a huge stumbling block. And You knew people could get distracted by belongings very easily. It was true when You walked the earth, and it's true today. It's definitely true in my own life. I admit I can get distracted by what I have and what I don't have. It's easy to want more or want something different, and it's easy to start obsessing over those wants. When I do that, I lose sight of how grateful I am for the things I actually do have. I forget to thank You for all You've given me. Please forgive me! You've blessed me in many ways, and I really am thankful for Your good gifts. I want to focus on those the next time I'm tempted to think greedy thoughts. In Your name I pray. Amen.

Rest on Every Side

The kingdom of Jehoshaphat was at peace,
for his God had given him rest on every side.
2 CHRONICLES 20:30 NIV

Father God, it really is amazing to realize that You give rest. Even when it seems like people could or should be against me, You have a way of working in my favor. You have the power to save and protect me. Unfortunately, it's easy for me to fall into the temptation to fear. I don't want to live my life being afraid of what could happen to me. I want to live with bold confidence that You will do what's best for me. When I fully believe that You're for me, I can live at peace. My soul will feel rested because I have nothing to fear. Thank You for the way You work in my life for my good. I'll be the first to admit I don't know how to make everyone at peace with me. In fact, sometimes I know I disappoint people or seem to attract conflict by the things I say or do. I'm so relieved I don't have to panic or try to do everything on my own. Please help me trust You more. Please work in my thoughts, words, and actions so I can be more of a peacemaker. In Jesus' name I pray. Amen.

Who Do I Honor?

They did know God, but they did not honor Him as God. They were not thankful to Him and thought only of foolish things. Their foolish minds became dark. They said that they were wise, but they showed how foolish they were. They gave honor to false gods that looked like people who can die and to birds and animals and snakes. This honor belongs to God Who can never die.

ROMANS 1:21–23 NLV

Father, so much in this world takes my attention away from You. When I see something I want, I spend a lot of time thinking about it. Sometimes I obsess about people. At other times I can't stop thinking about what I'd like to do in the future. I'm so easily distracted by these things and put a whole lot more importance on them than they actually deserve. In fact, sometimes I give more honor to these things and ideas than I give You. I know You, but I don't always honor You as God. At other times I think I deserve what I have and I forget to thank You, but You're the giver of all good gifts. Please help me see when I'm letting other things take Your place. I want to worship and honor You! Amen.

Your Unfailing Love

May your unfailing love be my comfort,
according to your promise to your servant.
PSALM 119:76 NIV

Lord, I try to find comfort in a lot of things. Sometimes I head straight to food or shopping. Other times I look to my friends' approval or social media responses. And still other times I try to find comfort by zoning out in front of a screen. None of those quick fixes actually brings lasting comfort. It may cheer me up for a little while or seem to numb my thoughts and feelings. But true, I-can-feel-it-deep-down comfort is found in Your unfailing, never-ending love. You've promised me a kind of love that will never let me go. Your love is patient and kind. Your love believes and hopes and endures. It's not jealous or proud or arrogant. Your love doesn't keep track of the times I let You down. It will remain forever and ever. I want Your love to comfort me when I feel restless or sad, angry or disappointed. I want Your love to fill up my heart and overflow into my thoughts and words. In Jesus' name I ask all this. Amen.

What Is Good?

He has shown you, O mortal, what is good. And what does the LORD require of you? To act justly and to love mercy and to walk humbly with your God.

MICAH 6:8 NIV

Lord God, opinions change so quickly in this world. It's hard to decide what I should or shouldn't do. Instead of basing my opinions on what other people tell me, I want to make my decisions based on what Your Word says I should do! Thank You for being so clear in the Old Testament book of Micah. I don't need to wonder what is good, and I don't need to wonder what You require of me. In all situations, I need to treat everyone justly. I need to love mercy all the time and seek it out. And I need to walk humbly with You. As I'm acting justly and loving mercy, I don't want to get all puffed up with pride. Please help me look for justice and treat others with mercy without even a hint of pride that I'm doing the right thing or obeying Your requirements. Thanks again for telling me what is good! In Jesus' name I pray. Amen.

Who Am I Trying to Please?

Am I now trying to win the approval of human beings, or of God? Or am I trying to please people? If I were still trying to please people, I would not be a servant of Christ.

GALATIANS 1:10 NIV

Lord, it's so hard not to try to please people. Throughout my entire life, I've been motivated by praise. If I try hard enough or do what other people ask me to do or look or act a certain way, I get praise. It's nice to find favor with others! But before I jump through everyone else's hoops, I need to slow down and remember I don't have to be a people pleaser. The One I really should focus on pleasing is You. It doesn't matter what my friends think. And my family's opinions don't matter as much as Yours. To be Your servant, I need to please You. No one else's approval really matters. Please help me remember this and stop being concerned about pleasing people. In Jesus' name I pray. Amen.

Being Kind to the Cruel

If the one who hates you is hungry,
feed him. If he is thirsty, give him water.
PROVERBS 25:21 NLV

Father, it's so hard to be kind to people who are cruel to me! I'd rather stay away from bullies. When people say mean things to me or about me, I get hurt and angry. When people go out of their way to do mean things to me or my friends, I want to get back in revenge. I get really upset when people pick on me or people I love. So when I read what Jesus taught about loving Your enemies, I feel uncomfortable. And when Proverbs teaches to feed Your enemy if he or she is hungry or give Your enemy water if he or she is thirsty, I don't like it. But even if I don't like it or it makes me squirm a little, it doesn't mean I shouldn't do it. I know it's the right thing to do. And even if it's really tough, I still need to obey. Please help me do what's really difficult but right. In Jesus' name I pray. Amen.

Choosing What's Hard but Right

Finally, brothers and sisters, rejoice! Strive
for full restoration, encourage one another,
be of one mind, live in peace. And the God
of love and peace will be with you.
2 CORINTHIANS 13:11 NIV

Oh Lord, it's so hard to live in peace with people. Especially when someone's hurt my feelings with the things they've said or done, I would rather hold a grudge. You don't ask me to do what comes naturally though. And You don't ask me to do what would make me feel comfortable. What I'm supposed to do, whether I'd like it or not, is to try to fully restore broken relationships. I need to live in peace with my friends and my enemies. I need to try to create unity and be of one mind, even with people who don't agree with me. I need to encourage others and rejoice. Father, I could whine and complain and tell You how much I really don't want to do this. Or I could choose to obey You and watch the way You pour out Your love and peace in my life. Please help me trust You completely! Amen.

Brokenhearted

*The LORD is close to the brokenhearted and
saves those who are crushed in spirit.*

PSALM 34:18 NIV

Father God, I absolutely hate the feeling of a broken
heart. When I feel so sad and disappointed and helpless,
it feels like my very spirit is crushed. Being heartbroken
hurts. You never intended for humans to deal with feelings
like this. Your creation was absolute perfection, and sin
entered the picture and dashed everything to pieces.
Even if broken hearts weren't part of Your original plan, I
still need to deal with those feelings. Please help me feel
Your comfort when I'm upset. I want to pour out all my
thoughts and feelings to You so You can take the pieces
of my heart and put them back together in a beautiful
way. Thank You for staying close to me, no matter what.
In Jesus' name I pray. Amen.

Taking My Punishment

*He was pierced for our transgressions, he was crushed
for our iniquities; the punishment that brought us
peace was on him, and by his wounds we are healed.*
ISAIAH 53:5 NIV

Lord Jesus, I don't deserve all You've done for me. You were pierced for the wrong things I've done. You were crushed for my sins. My punishment was given to You. You were wounded for me. So that I wouldn't have to suffer for my sins forever, You chose to bleed and die for me. I absolutely deserve the punishment for all I've done wrong. Yet You've willingly taken it, and I need only to accept Your punishment on my behalf. I'm so sorry for Your sacrifice yet so completely grateful and relieved. Thank You for sparing me from separation from You. Thank You for stepping in so I could live forever. Thank You for bringing me peace and healing. You are worthy of my praise! In Your name I pray. Amen.

Strength in Weakness

I receive joy when I am weak. I receive joy when people talk against me and make it hard for me and try to hurt me and make trouble for me. I receive joy when all these things come to me because of Christ. For when I am weak, then I am strong.

2 CORINTHIANS 12:10 NLV

Lord, joy seems like it should be an impossibility in the middle of tough times. Yet with You, anything is possible! When I'm weak, You can bring me joy. When people talk against me, You can fill me with Your joy. When other people try to make life hard for me and stir up trouble, I don't have to worry or cower in fear. You can bring me joy! Even when people try to hurt me with the awful things they say and do, I can still be filled with Your joy. I don't have to dread facing any of those really awful things because You've promised me joy in the middle of them all. As long as I know and trust and love You, You'll fill me with Your joy and strength. Even when I feel weak and helpless, You'll make me strong. That truly is amazing. Thank You!

Truth Instead of Lies

Wounds from a friend can be trusted,
but an enemy multiplies kisses.
PROVERBS 27:6 NIV

Father, sometimes when my friends tell me the truth, it hurts. I'm not talking about their opinions, which could change. I'm talking about what I know is true. I may not want to hear it, but I need to listen. Please help me keep an open heart and mind to what they say. As hard as it is for them to tell me, their confrontation is done in love and for my benefit. What I can't trust is when enemies flatter me just to try to make me feel better or to win my affection. Please help me know the difference between the two. As nice as compliments make me feel, I don't want to get wrapped up in them. Also, as hard as it is to be brutally honest with my friends, please help me know when I need to step in and be a truth teller. Please give me wisdom and the right words! In Jesus' name I pray. Amen.

Unexpected Kindness

"If your enemy is hungry, feed him; if he is thirsty,
give him something to drink. In doing this,
you will heap burning coals on his head."
ROMANS 12:20 NIV

Lord God, it's hard to treat my enemies with kindness! When they're mean to me, it's hard not to be mean in return. When they hurt my feelings, I want to hurt them too. When they insult me, I'd love to get revenge. But because I am Your daughter, You ask me to do things very differently than the rest of the world. You ask me to be kind to mean people. In fact, I should do nice things when people treat me badly. Why would I do this? Well, people expect paybacks for bad behavior. Revenge is expected. But if I choose to treat a mean person with kindness? Well, that's the best way to upset them. Your Word even describes it as heaping burning coals on their head. Please help me do what doesn't come naturally to me. Please help me to be kind, no matter what. In Jesus' name I pray. Amen.

My Safe Place

For You have been a safe place for me,
a tower of strength where I am safe
from those who fight against me.
PSALM 61:3 NLV

Father, I don't always feel like I'm safe. Whether it's feeling threatened by people I know or situations I wish I wasn't in, sometimes I do feel afraid. Other times I listen to what *might* happen and become scared. Maybe some of my danger is very real and maybe some of it is imagined, but it leaves me wrestling with fear and doubt. Could You please help me? When I've trusted in You, You've been a safe place for me. Even when people have set their minds to target me and fight against me, You've been my tower of strength. You keep me safe. I want to keep my focus on You. When I focus on the rest of the world and circumstances and other people, it's easy to start getting upset. It's easy to look around at what's happening and feel myself fill with fear. Please help me take a step back and look to You in worship. When I think of how awesome You are and remember that You have a greater plan, I don't have to worry. You can wipe all my fears away as I trust You completely. Thank You for filling me with Your peace! In Jesus' name I pray. Amen.

Right or Wrong?

"The Lord of All said, 'Do what is right and be kind and show loving-pity to one another.'"
ZECHARIAH 7:9 NLV

Jesus, Lord of all, when I decide to trust You and follow You, my life changes. I turn from my own way of doing things to Your way of doing things. Your way is really, really good. In fact, it's so much better than anything I can choose on my own. But it's different from things I might feel comfortable doing. For instance, You've said I need to do what's right. I need to be kind. I need to show mercy to other people. Those are all really good things, and I definitely want other people to be kind and full of mercy and forgiveness to me. But to live it out every day? It's hard! Sometimes I like holding grudges. I get grumpy and don't feel like being kind to everyone. At other times I'm tempted to do what's wrong. Even in all my temptation to do my own thing, please help me choose to follow You. Please help me choose what is right in Your eyes. In Your name I pray. Amen.

Choosing to Be Still

Be quiet and know that I am God. I will be honored
among the nations. I will be honored in the earth.
PSALM 46:10 NLV

Father God, when I think of all the trouble in the world
right now, it's easy to get caught up in worries and fear. I
could imagine what might happen and get really stressed
out. Or I could quiet my mind, be still, stop obsessing over
what-ifs, and know that You are God. You are the Lord of
all. You're above everything else, and nothing happens
that You don't allow to happen. You're the One who will
be honored among the nations and in the entire earth.
I won't be honored. Other people alive today won't be
honored. You *alone* will be honored. Because of that, I
don't have to stress about what's happening. I don't have
to be afraid. I just need to be still. When I'm quiet and
choose not to worry, I will remember and know that You
are God. Because of You, I can experience peace. Thank
You! In Jesus' holy and righteous name I pray. Amen.

Be My Light

*Do not gloat over me, my enemy! Though
I have fallen, I will rise. Though I sit in
darkness, the Lord will be my light.*
MICAH 7:8 NIV

O Lord, I know enemies are people created in Your image, just like me. But I don't like the way they treat me! I don't like how angry and hurt I feel when I deal with them! It seems like life would be better—or at least easier—without them. I need to remember that I can grow and become stronger because of their opposition. And even if I don't like the way they make me feel, You can use them to help me learn how not to treat people and how to deal with problems. Please be my light and guide my way. Even though it feels like I've fallen and can't get up, please help me rise and be stronger than ever. Even though it feels like I'm in the dark and can't see the right way to go, please light my way. I want to be Your representative in this world. In Jesus' name I pray. Amen.

Work for Peace

*Work for the things that make peace and help
each other become stronger Christians.*
ROMANS 14:19 NLV

Father God, peace doesn't come naturally. As much as I'd like to think people could get along peacefully, conflict and disagreements usually bring the opposite result. Even if other people try to argue or pick a fight with me, I can work for the things that make peace. Please help me overlook hurtful words and actions. Please help me to be kind even when people disagree with me. Please help me forgive even if and when I don't feel like it. Before I respond to insults or hurtful comments, please help me choose quiet. Could You please use my gentle responses and my attempts to be a peacemaker to help other people become stronger Christians? Whether people are watching my response or trying to pick a fight, I would love for the way I treat others to point them to You. Give me the strength and patience to do this work, please! In Jesus' name I pray. Amen.

Out of the Mud

He lifted me out of the slimy pit, out of the
mud and mire; he set my feet on a rock
and gave me a firm place to stand.

PSALM 40:2 NIV

Lord, sometimes it feels like I'm in the middle of a slimy pit here on earth. I feel like I'm slogging through really gross, really hard times. I can't seem to keep my footing very steady because I'm slipping and sliding, and I feel like I'm ready to fall on my face. But You have a way of pulling me out of this sloppy mess. You can lift me right out and set my feet on a firm rock. I can catch my breath and not worry about falling down. Thank You! Thanks for being my firm foundation. Thanks for being my steady, sturdy helper. I don't want to think of what my life would be like without You! In Jesus' name I pray. Amen.

No Matter What

*"For the mountains may be removed and the hills
may shake, But My favor will not be removed from
you, nor will My covenant of peace be shaken,"
says the LORD who has compassion on you.*
ISAIAH 54:10 NASB

O Lord, Your compassion for me is something I'll always be grateful for but will never fully understand. No matter what happens in this world, I can trust You and Your never-ending love for me. Your favor will continue no matter what. Your promise of peace won't change, even when it seems like all peace disappears in this world. Even if and when natural disasters happen all around me, I still can trust You and Your goodness. And if everything steady and reliable around me caves in, I still can trust in You. You're my rock! Your faithful love and protection are such good gifts. Thank You! I love You! In Jesus' name I pray. Amen.

Friend of God

It happened as the Holy Writings said it would happen.
They say, "Abraham put his trust in God and he became
right with God." He was called the friend of God.

JAMES 2:23 NLV

Father God, sometimes I wonder if I'm doing all I can to become right with You. Do I have to do something specific to be known by You? If I do certain things, will You turn against me? If I work hard at trying to be good, will You love me more? Instead of trying to wrestle through all these thoughts and figure things out on my own, I'm relieved I can go to Your Word for the answers and examples I need. Abraham was a man who was really important to You—he was the father of Your nation and Your friend. How did Abraham get all of these blessings and favors? He put his trust in You. Even when it seemed like everything was against him, He kept trusting in You and Your promises. That trust really was true faith in You. And that faith made him right with You. I want to put my trust in You! I want to live my life with an unshakable faith in You. In Jesus' holy, trustworthy name I pray. Amen.

Don't Be Scared!

"Have I not commanded you? Be strong and courageous! Do not be terrified nor dismayed, for the LORD your God is with you wherever you go."
JOSHUA 1:9 NASB

Lord, I'm afraid! When I think about what might happen to me or what I might face, I get scared. But my fears are based on what-ifs. What if something happens? What if my worst fears come true? Instead of fearing possibilities, I just need to focus on the reality of what's here and now. You haven't commanded me to be afraid. Instead, You've commanded me to be strong! And courageous! I don't have to be terrified or live in fear. I don't have to be discouraged. What I need to remember is that You're with me wherever I go. You're always with me! Knowing that the God of the universe is with me all the time to strengthen and guide me makes me feel brave. Thank You! Amen.

Freedom to Love

You, my brothers and sisters, were called to be free. But do not use your freedom to indulge the flesh; rather, serve one another humbly in love.

GALATIANS 5:13 NIV

Father, I am so thankful You've called me to be free! So much in this world tries to enslave me, whether it's people telling me what to do or rules I need to follow. I feel like I'm always trapped, trying to figure out what rules I need to obey. You have Your own rules, but they bring me life instead of consequences. They bring me freedom instead of tying me down. Because of my freedom in You and the way You love me so very much, I'd love to treat others the way You treat me. I'd love to reflect Your love to everyone! Please help me reach out and serve people in love. This means I need to make an effort—serving doesn't just happen automatically. But please help me use my freedom in You to serve in kindness instead of going crazy with sin and making myself happy. I'd love to make other people happy instead! Please help me serve others the way Jesus served. Amen.

Safe with Him

For You are my rock and my safe place. For the honor of Your name, lead me and show me the way.
PSALM 31:3 NLV

Lord God, You are my rock! You are my safe place! I can run to You when I'm afraid and it seems like my world comes crashing in. You're strong and steady and never changing. I am so thankful I can rely completely on You. Please lead me. In Your perfect wisdom, please show me the way to go. I want to do what You've planned for me, but I don't know what it is! Would You please guide me? Because I'm Yours, I know I don't have to fear. I can get excited about the unknowns in my future because You're in control. What a relief! Thank You for Your peace. In Jesus' name I pray. Amen.

Love and Kindness

"I led them with cords of human kindness, with ties of love. To them I was like one who lifts a little child to the cheek, and I bent down to feed them."

HOSEA 11:4 NIV

Lord, when I read the Bible and see the ways You love and lead Your people, it makes me feel all warm and fuzzy. You led the Israelites with cords of human kindness and ties of love. That means You were kind and gentle. You didn't drive Your people or force them to go Your way. There's nothing harsh about the way You guide. You compare Yourself to a kind, affectionate adult who lifts a child to His cheek or bends down to feed. You bring us to Your same level and don't talk down to us or treat us like we're unworthy to get Your care. You're God and You have the right to treat us any way You want. Knowing how You do treat humans, just like we're made in Your image, makes me know how much I mean to You. You are a good, good God, and I love You! Amen.

A Bunch of Belongings

We came into this world with nothing. For sure,
when we die, we will take nothing with us. If we
have food and clothing, let us be happy.
1 TIMOTHY 6:7–8 NLV

Father, I admit that I think about my belongings more than I probably should. I consider what clothes and shoes I want to wear. I have my favorite possessions that bring me comfort. I take a lot of time cleaning up my stuff because I have so much. And when I'm not focused on belongings or hobbies, I really like figuring out what to eat next. I like food! When I think about all of my favorite things and all that I have, I realize You've given me so much. Thank You! But as much as I like these things, they won't last forever. Just as I didn't bring a thing with me into this world when I was born, I won't take a thing out of this world when I die. All I have is myself. Please help me focus more on how I'm loving You and becoming a better me than on gathering a bunch of belongings. In Jesus' name I pray. Amen.

Help!

Listen to my prayer, O God. Do not hide Yourself from what I ask. Hear me and answer me. My thoughts trouble me and I have no peace, because of the voice of those who hate me and the power of the sinful. For they bring trouble upon me, and in anger they keep on having bad thoughts against me.

PSALM 55:1–3 NLV

Father, please listen to my prayer and help! I'm so upset with what's going on around me. People hate me for reasons I can't control. Their hate is bubbling over in their words, attitudes, and threats. I don't know what to do! It's like I can't get away from their anger. They're trying so hard to scare me just so I'll do what they want me to do, but I don't want to cave in. Their opinions aren't the only ones that matter in the world! I have my own thoughts. I have my own voice. I can make my own decisions. And as long as what I'm choosing glorifies You, I don't want other people to sway me. Please help me know how to respond to these angry people. Please help me treat them with respect even when they disrespect me. I want to do and say everything in love, even when I'm hated. I ask all of this in Jesus' name. Amen.

Peace Instead of Panic

"Peace I leave with you. My peace I give to you.
I do not give peace to you as the world gives.
Do not let your hearts be troubled or afraid."
JOHN 14:27 NLV

Lord Jesus, You knew You couldn't stay on earth forever. But before You left, You gave such a good gift to Your followers. You gave Your peace! Your peace is amazing. It's not like anything the world gives. It's not like You've ended an actual war or turned enemies into friends. You've given peace of mind and a peace I can feel deep inside. Your peace takes away my fear. With Your peace ruling my heart, I don't worry. When the world around me spins into panic at any possible danger, I can stay calm. It's such a relief that I don't have to blow everything into a huge disaster. I don't need to be a drama queen. I can rest in Your peace, and that makes my life feel so much better than a life of panic. Thank You! In Your name I pray. Amen.

Rest and Wait

Rest in the Lord and be willing to wait for Him.
Do not trouble yourself when all goes well with
the one who carries out his sinful plans.

PSALM 37:7 NLV

Oh Lord, waiting seems so hard! I admit I'm impatient. I want things to happen in my own timing. But You have a way of making me wait for Your right, perfect time. I don't have to rush things. In fact, I need to slow down and wait for You, even if that isn't enjoyable. Even when I feel like I could burst in anticipation, I want to choose to wait. I'll also admit it's hard for me to wait when I watch people around me getting the things I want. Those people don't wait for You. They do whatever feels right, or they go after anything they want without considering You and Your will. Please help me keep my eyes on You and not on them. When it's so hard to watch what they're doing and not feel jealous, please reassure me. When I want to do what I want in my own timing, please make me stop to wait for You. It might feel hard, but Your timing and Your way are the absolute best for me. I won't have any regrets when I wait for You. In Jesus' name I pray. Amen.

Going Out with Joy

"For you will go out with joy and be led in peace; the mountains and the hills will break into shouts of joy before you, and all the trees of the field will clap their hands."
ISAIAH 55:12 NASB

Lord, I like to imagine going out with joy and being led in peace. It sounds so happy to me. When I think about going places, I don't always go out with joy. In fact, sometimes I'm pretty grumpy or discouraged. And when I think of You leading me in peace, I realize how different it is when I try to lead myself. When I follow my own logic and decisions, I'm filled with doubts and worries. Please help me follow Your guidance. When I do, even nature will celebrate. But I have to admit that I'll wonder what's going on if the animals start singing and dancing with me! All kidding aside, thank You for all the reasons I have to be grateful. In Jesus' name I pray. Amen.

The Antidote to Worry

Do not worry. Learn to pray about everything. Give thanks to God as you ask Him for what you need.

PHILIPPIANS 4:6 NLV

Lord God, worrying comes so naturally. When I listen to what's happening in the world or wonder about what might happen in my future or to people I love, it's easy to start thinking about negative things that might happen. Why is it so easy to think about the worst possibilities? But because of You, I don't have to worry. If I'd just learn to pray about everything, You'd fill me with Your peace. Please help my faith in You grow and grow. Help me learn to trust You completely. Once my trust and faith in You do grow, I won't have a reason to worry. I want to notice the ways You work in my day and thank You for them. And I want to pray to You about any concern that comes to mind, whether it's something silly or serious. The more I pray, the more I'll trust You and the more my worries will disappear! In Jesus' name I pray. Amen.

Find the Good Way

This is what the LORD says: "Stand at the crossroads and look; ask for the ancient paths, ask where the good way is, and walk in it, and you will find rest for your souls. But you said, 'We will not walk in it.'"

JEREMIAH 6:16 NIV

Lord, there's so much noise in this world! So many different messages are being shouted at me. I want to find the good way, and I want to walk in it! If Your good way offers rest for my soul, I want it, even if it's different than anything the world offers. In the Old Testament, Jeremiah explained that Your good way could be found by looking and asking for it. Your good way is nothing new—in fact, it's ancient. But just because it's really old doesn't mean it's outdated. And it doesn't mean that I can't use it in my life. It's a lot like GPS in the way that it will guide me to the right destination. It will tell me the right way to go. That's exactly what I need. Thank You, Lord! Amen.

How Will You Be Found?

So then, dear friends, since you are looking forward to this, make every effort to be found spotless, blameless and at peace with him.
2 PETER 3:14 NIV

Lord Jesus, Your disciple Peter gave specific instructions for how Your followers should live: I need to be at peace with You. And I need to be spotless and blameless. Living a spotless and blameless life makes me nervous because I know I mess up every day. Sometimes I make unintentional mistakes, but other times I know what I'm doing wrong and choose to do it anyway. Please forgive me! I want to start making every effort to live in a way that reflects my love for You. I want to make You happy with the things I say and do. I don't want to feel nervous about my relationship with You. I want to choose what's right so I can be at peace with You. In Your name I pray. Amen.

Your Guide to the End

*This God is our God for ever and ever; he
will be our guide even to the end.*

PSALM 48:14 NIV

Father God, knowing You are God forever and ever makes
me realize how majestic and awesome You are. You always
have been God, and You always will be God. There's never
been a split second in all of eternity when You weren't
God. I can't understand it or explain it, but I'm in awe
of You! Knowing You'll willingly guide me is absolutely
amazing. You'll be my guide until the end—until I take my
last breath in this life. You're the Creator of all and Lord
of heaven and earth. And You willingly guide me. Thank
You! I pray I won't get in Your way. Please help me trust
and follow You. In Jesus' name I pray. Amen.

No Need to Fear

"Be strong and courageous, do not be afraid or in dread of them, for the LORD your God is the One who is going with you. He will not desert you or abandon you."

DEUTERONOMY 31:6 NASB

Lord, it's easy to get distracted by people who don't like me. When I remember the things they've said about me or done to me, I get upset. I don't want to fixate on negative thoughts. I don't want to live in fear. I don't want to continue judging others or having them invade my thoughts. I don't want to dread seeing or hearing them. Thank You for assuring me that You go with me. In fact, You go with me every day everywhere I go. I'm never alone. And no matter what, You won't abandon me. Thank You for that kind of caring concern! Thank You for that love and devotion! Because of You, I can be strong! I can be brave and full of courage. Because of You, I don't have to live in fear! In the strong name of Jesus I pray. Amen.

Being Sure

*Now faith is being sure we will get what we hope
for. It is being sure of what we cannot see.*
HEBREWS 11:1 NLV

Father, when I think about what it means to have faith in
something—or faith in You—I know it means that I have
complete trust and belief in something I can't physically
prove. I may not be able to see You right now. It's not like
I can introduce You to my friends so we can all sit around
and have a conversation with You. But I still know You're
there. You show Yourself in my life every day! When I look
for You, I find evidence of You working. In some ways,
You're like the wind. I may never be able to see the actual
wind, but I can see the effects of the wind. I can hear and
feel the wind. Just as I'm certain wind exists, I'm certain
You exist too. I'm sure of You! In Jesus' name I pray. Amen.

Don't Be a Hater

Do not be full of joy when the one who hates you
falls. Do not let your heart be glad when he trips.
PROVERBS 24:17 NLV

Father, You know I'm not always nice and kind. I may not be mean, but I take sides. I have favorite people. I know who I want to spend time with and who I'd rather avoid. I even have enemies. And I have a hard time forgiving people who make my life miserable. Help me reach way beyond myself and be kind to them. When they mess up and I'm tempted to celebrate, please stop me in my tracks. When they come into really hard times, please stop me from being glad. Somehow, with Your amazing, godly powers, please change my heart so I even feel sorry for them. Even if I will never truly be their friend, please help me show way more compassion to them than I feel I can. Please work through me. In Jesus' holy name I pray. Amen.

His Resting Favor

*"Glory to God in the highest heaven, and on
earth peace to those on whom his favor rests."*
LUKE 2:14 NIV

Lord Jesus, when You were born, the angels came to announce Your birth with great joy and praise. As they celebrated Your birth, they gave glory to God. They also wished peace to those people on earth on whom God's favor rests. Because Your favor rests on me, I praise You and believe in You and trust You as my Lord and my God. That's amazing to comprehend! Even if I feel like my life is a teensy blip in the scope of eternity, it matters to You. Your favor rests on me, and I get to experience true peace. I want that truth and Your love to propel me to do big things for You. I want to celebrate You with joy and loud praise, just like the angels! In Your name I pray. Amen.

His Song

By day the LORD directs his love, at night his
song is with me—a prayer to the God of my life.

PSALM 42:8 NIV

Lord God, the way You love and care for me is breathtakingly beautiful. I really can't comprehend just how very much You love me. But by day, You direct Your love for me in a million different ways. You work behind the scenes so I don't even realize all the ways You're lovingly working things out for my best. You're directing me with Your love. And at night when I feel so alone, You're right there with me, comforting me with Your song. Your song is with me all night long, and even if I couldn't name the tune or the words, my heart knows it completely. And as my heart sings along, it's a prayer to You. Realizing that I'm never alone is such a comfort. Remembering that You're here to comfort and guide and love me is a great relief! You fill me with Your perfect peace, and for that I am thankful. I love and trust You with my whole heart! Amen.

Crooked or Straight

They do not know the way of peace, and there is no justice in their tracks; they have made their paths crooked, whoever walks on them does not know peace.

ISAIAH 59:8 NASB

Father, I could go down very different paths in this life. One path is what You've planned and established for my own good and is filled with peace. Another path is what I choose to create on my own. This path doesn't always have the clearest direction. It gets me somewhere eventually, but it's a very different destination than I intended. Yet another path is what the world lays out before me. This path skips right past any justice, winds around in crooked, twisting directions, and leads me to a place of regret. As fun as the world's path might seem, and as much as my own path seems totally focused on me, I'd really like to feel at peace. I don't want to have to worry about anything. I want to trust that You have everything handled. Having You guide me on Your perfect path of peace sounds pretty great to me! In Jesus' name I pray. Amen.

Why Worry?

"Do not worry about tomorrow. Tomorrow will have its own worries. The troubles we have in a day are enough for one day."
MATTHEW 6:34 NLV

Lord, most days I could worry about a lot of things! From things in my own life to problems my friends and family face, I have a lot of concerns. When I add in my school and what's going on in my community and what might happen in the world, I end up thinking about worry after worry. Jesus taught that I shouldn't worry about tomorrow. That means I don't need to worry about what might happen in the future. What I can spend time thinking and praying about is what's going on today. Please help me focus on what's going on here and now. Please show me how I can trust You and follow You in the decisions I make today so I won't worry about tomorrow. In Jesus' name I pray. Amen.

Living with Honor

"My agreement with him [Levi] was one of life and peace, and I gave them to him, that he might honor Me with fear. So he honored Me with fear. My name filled him with fear and wonder. True teaching was in his mouth, and no wrong was found on his lips. He walked with Me in peace and was right and good. And he turned many from sin."

MALACHI 2:5-6 NLV

Father, Your prophet Malachi told the Israelites about many things that upset You. The Israelite priests came from the tribe of Levi, but they wandered from Levi's example. Levi lived a life that honored You with fear and wonder. He told the truth, did what was right and good, walked with You in peace, and turned other people away from sin. I'll never be a priest, but I can still look to Levi's example. I'd love to honor You. I want to turn people away from sin and teach Your truth. I want to be honest and do what's right and good. Above all else, I want to walk with You in peace. It may not always be easy to do this, especially when I'm tempted by things of the world or things I'd like, but please give me the strength to do this. I love You! I fear You. And I want to honor You. In Jesus' holy name I pray. Amen.

Live Like I Believe

We know God's Son has come. He has given us the understanding to know Him Who is the true God. We are joined together with the true God through His Son, Jesus Christ. He is the true God and the life that lasts forever.

1 JOHN 5:20 NLV

Father God, thank You for helping me understand what truth is. So many people in this world don't know! They wander around believing every little thing and end up wrestling with doubt. You've let me know and understand Your truth. You've filled me with peace and certainty by revealing to me why Your Son came into the world. He is the true God. Through Jesus, You give me life that lasts forever. Thank You! Thank You for the way Jesus joins me together with You. Thank You that all I need to do is believe the truth that Jesus is Your Son who lived a perfect life, died on a cross for my sin, and triumphed over death three days later. When I trust in Him, You give me forever life with You. I believe, Lord! Please help me to live like it! In Jesus' name I pray. Amen.

A Glad Heart

My heart is glad. My soul is full of joy.
My body also will rest without fear.

PSALM 16:9 NLV

Lord, because of You, my heart is glad. You fill my soul with joy! When I see the way You work in my life and think of all You've done for me, I'm so happy! I'm also relieved that I can fully rest without any fear. Living with complete trust in You and seeing the way You work wonderful things in my life fills me with joy. Thank You! Thank You for the way You're for me and not against me. Thank You for the way You give me good gifts time after time. I'm so thankful I can find my full soul rest in You. I want my love and joy for You to shine in my life so others can come to know You too. Please use my life to bring others closer to You. In Jesus' name I pray. Amen.

Show Me!

Show me your ways, LORD, teach me your paths.
Guide me in your truth and teach me, for you are
God my Savior, and my hope is in you all day long.
PSALM 25:4–5 NIV

Father God, my hope is in You all day long. From the time I wake up until the time I fall asleep, I'm glad I can trust in You completely. I admit that I get confused in this life. Please straighten out my thoughts and give me clarity so I don't have to feel muddled. I want to follow You. Could You please show me Your ways? And could You please teach me Your paths? I have a hard time figuring it all out on my own, so I'd really love for You to help me. Guide me in Your truth, please. I want to read Your Word more and more so I know what Your truth is. When I do read the Bible, please teach me in the way only You can. I'm so thankful that You are my God and Savior. It's in Jesus' name I ask all of this. Amen.

Scripture Index

Genesis
39:6. 36

Exodus
13:21. 26
15:13. 46

Deuteronomy
31:6 176

Joshua
1:9 163
1:13. 23
21:44 73

Judges
18:6 33

1 Samuel
20:42 136

2 Samuel
22:34. 88

1 Kings
5:4. 123

1 Chronicles
22:9. 83

2 Chronicles
15:7 16
20:30 143

Job
6:14 56
11:13, 17–18. 18

Psalms
3:3. 25
4:8. 45
6:3. 80
8:3–4. 10
14:2 75
16:9 185
17:8–9 28
18:3. 58
18:6 38
18:17. 135
19:7 140
25:1–2 68
25:4–5. 186
27:14 130
29:11. 15

31:3 165
31:24 100
32:7 30
33:20–22 20
34:4 50
34:14 35
34:18 150
35:20 85
37:7 170
37:11 65
37:37 120
40:2 160
40:5 90
42:8 180
46:1–3 127
46:10 157
48:14 175
55:1–3 168
59:1–2 48
59:17 105
61:3 155
62:1–2 95
71:20–21 98
73:28 70
78:35–37 60
84:11–12 40
85:8 55

119:50 125
119:76 145
119:165 110
127:2 115

Proverbs
3:13–15 118
4:26 78
8:11 8
12:20 63
16:7 133
16:22 116
17:1 93
17:17 66
24:17 178
25:21 148
27:6 153
27:9 86

Ecclesiastes
9:17 103

Isaiah
25:1 138
26:3 53
26:12 121
30:15 101

32:17 131
32:18 111
35:4. 108
40:11 11
40:28-29 31
41:10 61
41:13. 71
43:1-3 21
48:18. 81
49:13 96
52:7 141
53:5. 151
54:10. 161
55:12 171
57:15 91
57:18 41
59:8. 181

Jeremiah
6:16 173
17:8 13
31:13. 51

Daniel
10:19 76

Hosea
10:12 106
11:4. 166

Micah
5:4. 128
6:8. 146
7:8. 158

Zephaniah
3:17 113

Zechariah
7:9 156
8:16 43

Malachi
2:5-6. 183

Matthew
5:14-16. 104
5:43-44 124
6:19-21. 126
6:25. 39
6:27. 102
6:34. 182
10:19 49

11:28–29 7
11:29 77

Mark
1:16–18 107
6:31 87

Luke
1:78–79 12
2:14 179
6:37 54
10:40–42 42
12:15 142
24:38 82

John
7:24 64
14:1 92
14:27 169
16:13 22
21:22 74

Romans
1:21–23 144
5:1 9
8:6 79
12:20 154

14:19 159
15:13 69

1 Corinthians
2:4–5 97
14:33 19

2 Corinthians
1:3–4 37
10:12 44
12:9 67
12:10 152
13:11 149

Galatians
1:10 147
5:13 164
5:22–23 52

Ephesians
2:17 139

Philippians
1:6 14
1:20 32
4:6 172
4:7 89

4:11 112

Colossians
3:12 62
3:15 59

1 Thessalonians
5:23 129

2 Thessalonians
2:16–17 17
3:16 119

1 Timothy
2:1–2 27
6:7–8 167

2 Timothy
2:22 109

Hebrews
6:19–20 24
4:9–10 47
11:1 177
12:1–2 114
12:14 99
13:5 132

James
2:23 162
3:18 84
4:4 34
4:12 122

1 Peter
3:4 57
3:11 94
3:14 72

2 Peter
3:14 174

1 John
5:11–12 117
5:20 184

Jude
1:1–2 29

Revelation
7:9–10 134
7:11–12 137